A

CHRONOLOGICAL HISTORY

OF THE

CIVIL WAR IN AMERICA.

ILLUSTRATED WITH

A. J. JOHNSON'S AND J. H. COLTON'S

Steel Plate Maps and Plans

OF THE

SOUTHERN STATES AND HARBORS.

A WORK FOR THE MILLIONS.

BY

RICHARD SWAINSON FISHER, M.D.,

EDITOR OF "COLTON'S GENERAL ATLAS OF THE WORLD;" "COLTON'S CABINET ATLAS OF THE WORLD;" "JOHNSON'S FAMILY ATLAS OF THE WORLD;" "THE BOOK OF THE WORLD," ETC., ETC.; AND LATE EDITOR OF THE JOURNAL OF THE AMERICAN GEOGRAPHICAL AND STATISTICAL SOCIETY.

COMPLETE TO DATE.

NEW YORK:

JOHNSON AND WARD, PUBLISHERS,

No. 86 CEDAR STREET.

1863.

PUBLISHERS' ADVERTISEMENT.

We present to the public a Chronological History of the Civil War in America, from its inauguration, in the secession of South Carolina from the Union, on the 20th December, 1860, to the 1st January, 1863. This volume is a chronicle of the most important political and military events which have marked, for the past two years, the history of the United States. As its title imports, it is chronological. Events are narrated in the order of their occurrence from day to day. The time has not yet come for the philosophy of history, in regard to this war: to lay bare the secret springs of action, for too many are interested in their concealment; to trace the influence of ordinances and battles, diplomacy and decrees, upon civilization and human progress, for these elements have but begun to operate. Both civilian and soldier will find this a most useful publication upon the war.

In selecting from the vast amount of material accumulated for such a work, the utmost care has been taken that unauthenticated or theoretical assumptions might not find a record as facts. The compiler, indeed, has relied altogether on official and other well-attested documents for information. The results—recorded without gloss or fanciful embellishment—stand as historical truths.

We need not enlarge upon the contents of such a work. It embraces all that is now essential upon the subject treated. It is not partisan in its tone. It deals only in facts; and whether victory or defeat, success or repulse, crown one or other of the contestants, the record is made without partiality. In such a work no other course could have been pursued without manifest injury to the truth of history. In its pages the despondent may find reason for hope, and the sanguine a vindication of their faith in a glorious future for their country.

To give greater interest to the volume, the publishers have added an "Appendix," in which will be found the Ordinances of Secession from the Federal Union of the several rebel States, the more important Proclamations of the President of the United States, and a number of valuable statistics relating to the population and resources of the Union, the expenditures of the government on account of the war, and other matters to which reference is made in the body of the book. In the chronicle under date January 1, 1863, will be found statements of the debts contracted by the contestants for war purposes up to that time.

Accurate maps accompany the volume, and will be found invaluable as carefully prepared charts of the fields on which the contending armies have been and are now engaged.

Should the war be continued, an annual volume, similar in character to the present issue, will be prepared and published early after the close of each succeeding year. The volume for 1863 is now in the hands of the compiler, who is recording events as they occur, and while still fresh in memory—the only sure method of noting them with accuracy.

New York, 19*th March*, 1863.

CHRONOLOGICAL HISTORY

OF

THE CIVIL WAR IN AMERICA.

Rebellion and Secession, long threatened and determined upon by the slaveholding section of the United States, became realities in 1860. The issue was decided by the election of Abraham Lincoln to the Presidency of the United States. No sooner was the result of the election known than preparations were made for the separation of all the Southern States from the Union. The first public act which took place, having for its ultimate object the dissolution of existing political relations and the formation of a Southern Confederacy, was the call for a State Convention in South Carolina. This resulted in the secession of that State and subsequently of the other States now represented in the Confederate Congress. The progress of events since the date of this primary act is briefly but fully and accurately recorded in the following pages:

November, 1860.

10. Bill to raise and equip 10,000 volunteers for the defense of the State introduced into the South Carolina Legislature.

James Chestnut, senator from South Carolina, resigned his seat in the U. S. Senate.

South Carolina Legislature ordered the election of a State Convention to consider the question of secession.

11. James H. Hammond, senator from South Carolina, resigned his seat in the U. S. Senate.

15. Hon. Alex. H. Stevens, in a speech delivered at Milledgeville, Ga., spoke in opposition to secession, but favored a State Convention.

16. Great public meeting at Mobile and adoption of the famous Declaration of the Causes of Secession.

Governor of Virginia called an extra session of the State Legislature.

U. S. Senator Robert Toombs spoke in reply to Mr. Stevens at Milledgeville, Ga., advocating secession; and in a few days subsequently Mr. Stevens gave in his adhesion thereto.

17. Great public meeting at Charleston, S. C., at which the causes and rights of secession were discussed.

18. Georgia Legislature voted $1,000,000 for the purpose of arming the State, and ordered an election for delegates to a State Convention.

Major Anderson ordered to Fort Moultrie, harbor of Charleston, to relieve Col. Gardiner, ordered to Texas.

19. Governor of Louisiana ordered an extra session of the State Legislature.

20–23. Suspension of specie payments by the banks of Richmond, Baltimore, Washington, Philadelphia, and Trenton, and throughout the Southern States.

24. Vigilance associations organized in South Carolina. [Similar associations were subsequently organized in all the slave States, and thousands of Northern families were driven out of the country with threats and often with personal violence.]

29. Vermont Legislature refused, by a vote of 125 to 58, to repeal the Personal Liberty Bill.

Mississippi Legislature voted to send commissioners to confer with the authorities of the other slave-holding States.

December, 1860.

1. Florida Legislature voted to hold a State Convention and ordered an election for delegates thereto.

3. A John Brown anniversary meeting in Boston, Mass., broken up.

Opening of the 2d Session of the XXXVIth Congress. President Buchanan in his message denied the right of any State or States to secede. This assertion was fiercely attacked by Senator Clingman, of North Carolina, and as valiantly defended by Senator Crittenden, of Kentucky.

4. President Buchanan sent Mr. Trescott to South Carolina to request a postponement of hostile action until Congress could decide upon remedies.

Senator Iverson, of Georgia, in a speech delivered in the U. S. Senate, predicted the secession of five if not eight States before 4th March proximo. He was replied to by Senator Saulsbury, of Delaware, who spoke for the Union and reproved Iverson.

5. Election of delegates to a State Convention in South Carolina: all the candidates were for immediate secession.

6. Hon. John Bell, of Tennessee, published a letter in which he advocated the cause of the Union.

Democratic State Convention in Maryland: resolutions passed deploring the hasty action of South Carolina.

The House Committee of Thirty-Three announced by the Speaker: 16 Republicans and 17 Opposition.

10. Howell Cobb, U. S. Sec. of the Treasury, resigned, and was succeeded by Philip F. Thomas, of Maryland.

Senator C. C. Clay, of Alabama, resigned his seat in the U. S. Senate.

Louisiana Legislature, convened at Baton Rouge in extra session, voted to elect a State Convention, and appropriated $500,000 to arm the State.

General debate on the state of the country commenced in Congress.

13. Great Union demonstration in Philadelphia.

Extra session of the cabinet on the question of reinforcing Fort Moultrie: the President opposed it and carried his point.

14. Lewis Cass, U. S. Sec. of State, resigned and was succeeded by Jeremiah S. Black, of Pennsylvania. The cause of Gen. Cass' resignation was the refusal of the President to reinforce Fort Moultrie.

17. South Carolina State Convention assembled at Columbia: Gov. Pickens took ground for immediate secession.

Senator Wade, in a speech delivered in the U. S. Senate, foreshadowed the policy of the administration of President Lincoln.

18. The famous Crittenden Compromise introduced into the U. S. Senate. It was this: To renew the Missouri line of 36° 30′; prohibit slavery north and permit it south of that line; admit new States with or without slavery, as their constitutions provide; prohibit Congress from abolishing slavery in States, and in the District of Columbia so long

as it exists in Maryland and Virginia; permit free transmission of slaves by land or water in any State; pay for fugitive slaves rescued after arrest; repeal the inequality of commissioners' fees in the Fugitive Slave Act, and ask the repeal of Personal Liberty Bills in the Northern States. These concessions to be submitted to the people as amendments of the Constitution, and if adopted never to be changed.

18. Jacob Thompson, U. S. Sec. of the Interior, went to Raleigh to persuade the North Carolina Legislature to vote for secession.

19. Senator Johnson, of Tennessee, made a strong Union speech on the Crittenden Bill.

Gov. Hicks, of Maryland, refused to receive the Mississippi commissioner. The commissioner addressed a secession meeting in Baltimore.

20. South Carolina State Convention adopted a secession ordinance by a unanimous vote, the news of which was heard with enthusiasm throughout the Southern States.

The Committee of Thirteen appointed by the President of the Senate.

Hon. Caleb Cushing reached Charleston with a message from President Buchanan, guaranteeing that Major Anderson should not be reinforced, and asking the Convention to respect the federal laws. Convention refused to make any promises, and Mr. Cushing returned after a stay of five hours.

22. North Carolina Legislature adjourned: a bill to arm the State failed to pass the House.

The Crittenden Compromise propositions voted down in the Senate Committee of Thirteen.

23. Robbery of the Indian Trust Fund discovered at

Washington. Floyd, the Sec. of War, was the chief agent in this transaction.

24. South Carolina members of Congress present their resignation: the Speaker would not recognize it, and their names were called through the Session.

Election for State Convention in Alabama—result, a majority of upward of 60,000 for secession. A strong Union feeling was manifested in the northern counties.

People of Pittsburg, Pa., intercepted the shipment of ordnance from the arsenal to the Southern forts.

South Carolina State Convention adopted a "Declaration of Causes" for secession, and formally perfected the withdrawal of the State from the Union. An address to the slaveholding States adopted.

25. South Carolina State Convention adopted resolutions having in view the formation of a confederate government of the slaveholding States.

26. Commissioners from South Carolina arrived in Washington.

Major Anderson abandoned Fort Moultrie, and with his force, about 80 men, established himself in Fort Sumter.

27. Gov. Magoffin called an extra session of the Legislature of Kentucky.

Great excitement in Charleston on the discovery that Major Anderson had transferred his force to Sumter: troops were ordered out, and aid was tendered from Georgia and other States.

Revenue cutter "Aiken" treacherously surrendered to the South Carolina authorities.

28. Custom-house, post-office, and arsenal at Charleston seized by the authorities, and Castle Pinckney and Fort Moultrie occupied by the State troops.

29. John B. Floyd, U. S. Sec. of War, resigned, charging the President, by refusing to withdraw Major Anderson, with trying to provoke civil war. Real cause: fear of prosecution for robbing the Indian Trust Fund.

South Carolina Commissioners formally sought an audience of the President.

30. The President, in reply to the application of the South Carolina Commissioners, refused to receive them.

Joseph Holt, of Kentucky, appointed Secretary of War, in place of Floyd resigned.

31. The Senate Committee of Thirteen report that they have not been able to agree upon any general plan of adjustment, and lay their journal before the Senate.

South Carolina State Convention adopted an oath of abjuration and allegiance, and sent commissioners to the other slave States with a view to the formation of a Southern Confederacy.

January, 1861.

1. The frigate "Brooklyn" and another war vessel ordered to Charleston.

2. Fort Macon at Beaufort, the works at Wilmington, and the U. S. Arsenal at Fayetteville seized by the authorities of North Carolina.

The Legislature of Delaware passed a joint resolution in opposition to secession.

Forts Pulaski and Jackson, in the harbor of Savannah, and the U. S. Arsenal at Savannah seized by the Georgia State troops.

3. The South Carolina Commissioners left Washington on their return home, the President having returned unopened their last communication.

4. National Fast—this day was devoted to humiliation, fasting, and prayer, in accordance with the recommendation of the President.

Fort Morgan at the mouth of Mobile Bay and the U. S. Arsenal at Mobile seized by order of the Governor of Alabama.

Governor Pickens, of South Carolina, appointed his cabinet ministers, viz., Sec. of State, A. G. Magrath; Sec. of War, D. F. Jamison; Sec. of the Treasury, C. G. Memminger; Sec. of the Interior, A. C. Garlington, and Postmaster-General, W. W. Harllee.

4. South Carolina State Convention appointed *seven* delegates to "The General Congress of the Seceding States."

5. South Carolina State Convention adjourned, subject to the call of its President.

Steamer "Star of the West" sailed from New York with supplies and reinforcements for Fort Sumter.

Gov. Hicks, of Maryland, published a strong Union address to the people, refusing to call a convention.

Florida State Convention met at Tallahassee.

7. The Legislature of Virginia convened at Richmond.

State Convention of Alabama convened at Montgomery.

State Convention of Mississippi convened at Jackson.

Legislature of Tennessee convened at Nashville.

Senator Toombs, of Georgia, made a violent secession speech in the U. S. Senate.

Major Anderson's course in evacuating Fort Moultrie sustained by the House of Representatives.

State Convention of Florida passed a secession ordinance (62 *v.* 7).

8. Jacob Thompson, U. S. Sec. of the Interior, resigned after betraying the sailing of the "Star of the West" to reinforce Fort Sumter.

Forts Caswell and Johnson seized by the State troops of North Carolina.

9. The steamer "Star of the West" arrived off Charleston and was fired upon and driven back to sea by the rebel batteries of Morris Island and Fort Moultrie.

State Convention of Mississippi passed an ordinance for immediate secession (84 *v.* 15).

Steamer "Marion," of the New York and Charleston line, seized at Charleston by the State authorities. Released on the 11th.

10. State Convention of Florida passed an ordinance of secession (62 *v.* 7).

Forts St. Philip and Jackson, on the Mississippi, and Fort Pike, on Lake Pontchartrain, together with the U. S. Arsenal at Baton Rouge, seized by the State troops of Louisiana.

The President transmitted a special message to Congress on the affairs of the country.

11. State Convention of Alabama passed an ordinance of secession (61 *v.* 39).

Philip F. Thomas, of Maryland, appointed Sec. of the U. S. Treasury 11th Dec., 1860, resigned, and John A. Dix, of New York, appointed in his place.

Legislature of New York voted to tender the whole military power of the State to the President for the support of the Constitution.

12. Steamer "Star of the West" returned to New

York, having two shot-holes in her hull, received while in Charleston Harbor.

Five representatives from Mississippi (Singleton, Barkesdale, Davis, McRae, and Lamar) withdrew from Congress.

13. Fort Barrancas and the U. S. Navy Yard at Pensacola surrendered to the Florida and Alabama State troops.

14. Legislature of South Carolina declared that any attempt to reinforce Fort Sumter would be an act of war.

Ohio House of Representatives (58 *v.* 31) refused to pass a bill to repeal the "Act to prevent kidnapping," known as the Personal Liberty Bill.

15. Bill for calling a State Convention in Virginia passed by the Legislature—in the Senate by a vote of 45 to 1, and in the House of Representatives unanimously.

Secession meeting in New York.

16. The Crittenden Compromise in the United States Senate practically voted down by the adoption of Senator Clark's substitute, "that the Constitution is good enough, and secession ought to be put down."

Legislature of Arkansas voted to submit the question of a State Convention to the people.

Legislature of Missouri voted to hold a State Convention.

Col. Hayne, in the name of the Governor of South Carolina, demanded of the President the surrender of Fort Sumter. The President refused to receive him in any official capacity.

State Convention of Georgia assembled at Milledgeville.

17. Joseph Holt, of Kentucky, nominated Secretary of War.

18. Legislature of Massachusetts tendered to the President all the power of the State to support the Federal Government.

Legislature of Virginia appropriated $1,000,000 for the defense of the State.

19. State Convention of Georgia adopted an ordinance of secession (208 *v.* 89).

Legislature of Tennessee voted to call a State Convention.

21. Jefferson Davis, of Mississippi, Benjamin Fitzpatrick and C. C. Clay, Jr., of Alabama, and David L. Yulee and Stephen R. Mallory, of Florida, formally withdrew from the U. S. Senate.

The Alabama members (Houston, Moore, Clapton, Pugh, Curry, and Stallworth) withdrew from Congress.

22. Sherrard Clemens, of Virginia, made a strong Union speech in Congress.

Arms destined for Alabama seized in New York.

23. The Georgia members (Love, Crawford, Hardeman, Gartrell, Underwood, Jackson, and Jones) left the House of Representatives. Joshua Hill, also one of the Georgia representatives, refused to go with the others, but formally tendered his resignation.

Mr. Etheridge, of Tennessee, in a speech before Congress, declared secession to be rebellion, and to be put down at any cost.

Louisiana State Convention convened at Baton Rouge.

Second seizure of arms in New York.

24. U. S. Arsenal at Augusta, Ga., seized by the State troops.

Annual meeting of the Massachusetts Anti-Slavery Society broken up by a mob.

25. Legislature of Rhode Island repealed the Personal Liberty Bill.

26. Louisiana State Convention adopted an ordinance of secession (113 *v.* 17).

28. Texas State Convention convened at Austin.

29. Georgia State Convention adjourned to reassemble in Savannah on the call of its President.

Alabama State Convention adjourned to reassemble on the 4th March.

30. Grand Jury of District of Columbia presented charges against John B. Floyd, late Sec. of War, for maladministration in office and conspiracy against the government.

Legislature of North Carolina passed a bill submitting the question of a State Convention to the people—the first recognition in the seceding States that the people had any right to a voice in the matter.

U. S. revenue cutters "Cass" and "McClelland" surrendered to the Louisiana State authorities.

Kansas admitted into the Union as a non-slaveholding State.

31. U. S. Mint and Custom House at New Orleans seized by the State authorities.

February, 1861.

1. Texas State Convention passed an ordinance of secession (166 *v.* 7), to be submitted to the people on the 23d inst., and unless rejected by a majority vote, to take effect from the 2d March.

4. A peace convention, consisting of delegates from Virginia, Maryland, Kentucky, Tennessee, North Carolina, New York, Ohio, Missouri, New Jersey, Pennsylvania, Indiana, Illinois, Connecticut, New Hampshire, Vermont, Delaware, Rhode Island, and Massachusetts, convened in Washington: John Tyler, of Virginia, presided.

Convention of Delegates from the seceded States met at Montgomery to organize a confederate government. Howell Cobb was chosen chairman.

Election held in Virginia for delegates to State Convention. A large majority of members chosen were Union men, and the vote on the question of referring the action of the Convention back to the people resulted in a majority of 56,000 in favor of such reference.

5. John Slidell and Judah P. Benjamin, senators from Louisiana, withdrew from the U. S. Senate, and Taylor, Davidson, and Landrum, representatives (under instructions from the State Convention), from the House of Representatives. Bouligny, the member from New Orleans, announced that he would not obey the instructions.

6. Senator Johnson, of Tennessee, delivered an important speech in the U. S. Senate.

7. New Orleans was illuminated and pelican flags displayed in honor of secession.

8. The Montgomery Convention adopted the Constitution of the United States, with alterations chiefly relating to slavery and state rights, as the provisional constitution of the Confederate States of America.

Col. Hayne, commissioner from South Carolina,

unable to get recognition from the President, left Washington.

The Governor of Georgia seized several New York vessels in Savannah Harbor in retaliation for the seizure of arms in New York. The vessels were released on the 10th.

Little Rock (Ark.) Arsenal seized by the State authorities.

9. Jefferson Davis, of Mississippi, and Alexander H. Stevens, of Georgia, elected Provisional President and Vice-President of the Confederate States for one year by the Convention at Montgomery, Ala.

U. S. $25,000,000 loan bill signed by the President.

11. Abraham Lincoln, President-Elect of the United States, left Springfield, Ill., and commenced his journey to Washington.

U. S. House of Representatives "*Resolved:* That neither Congress nor the people or governments of the non-slaveholding States have a constitutional right to legislate upon or interfere with slavery in any slaveholding State of the Union."

12. The Confederate States government took charge of all questions pending between the States composing it and the United States government.

13. The electoral vote for President and Vice-President of the United States counted in Congress—

Vote for President.		Vote for Vice-President.	
Lincoln	180	Hamlin	180
Breckinridge	72	Lane	72
Bell	39	Everett	39
Douglas	12	Johnson	12

Virginia State Convention met at Richmond.

18. Jefferson Davis inaugurated Provisional President of the Confederate States at Montgomery.

People of Arkansas voted on the question of a State

Convention. Result — for 27,412, and against 15,826.

19. Enthusiastic reception of the President-Elect in New York city.

Fort Kearney, in Kansas, taken by the secessionists, but soon after retaken.

21. Jefferson Davis appointed his cabinet ministers, viz., Sec. of State, Toombs; Sec. of the Treasury, Memminger, and Sec. of War, L. P. Walker.

Governor of Georgia made another seizure of New York vessels.

President-Elect in Philadelphia.

22. 129th anniversary of the birthday of George Washington celebrated with great pomp and show throughout the loyal States.

23. President-Elect passes through Baltimore secretly, in order to prevent anticipated outrage in that city.

Secession ordinance of Texas voted on by the people and adopted by 24,000 majority.

25. Information received of the surrender and treason of Major-General Twiggs in Texas. Fort Brown was saved through the refusal of Capt. Hill to obey Twiggs' order.

27. Peace Convention submitted to the Senate their plan for pacification, and adjourned *sine die.* The principal article proposed the parallel 36° 30′ as a division between freedom and slavery in the Territories.

28. President Davis vetoed the bill legalizing the African Slave Trade.

Vote in the House of Representatives on the report of the Committee of Thirty-Three: resolutions adopted, 136 to 53.

Election in North Carolina to decide on the question of holding a State Convention, and to choose delegates thereto. Vote: for Convention 46,409, and against, 46,603.

March, 1861.

1. General Twiggs dismissed from the army of the United States for treason.
2. U. S. revenue cutter "Dodge" surrendered to the rebel authorities at Galveston.

   Tariff bill signed by the President.
4. Abraham Lincoln inaugurated President of the United States.

   Texas State Convention declared the State out of the Union.

   Alabama State Convention reassembled at Montgomery.

   Amendment to the Constitution of the United States, which passed the House 28th February, passed the Senate (24 *v.* 12).

   XXXVIth Congress closed.

   Arkansas State Convention convened at Little Rock.
5. Gen. Beauregard ordered to take command of the rebels at Charleston.

   U. S. Senate, in extra executive session, confirmed the nominations of President Lincoln for cabinet officers as follows:

State..W. H. Seward, *N. Y.*	Interior.........C. B. Smith, *Ind.*
Treas..S. P. Chase, *Ohio.*	Post-office.......M. Blair, *Md.*
War ..S. Cameron, *Pa.*	and—
Navy..G. Wells, *Ct.*	Attorney-Gen ...E. Bates, *Mo.*

6. C. S. Senate confirmed the nominations of President Davis for cabinet officers as follows:

State. R. Toombs, *Ga.*	Navy........S. R. Mallory, *Fla.*
Treas. C. L. Memminger, *S.C.*	Post-office ...J. H. Reagan, *Tex.*
War..L. P. Walker, *Ala.*	Attorney-Gen. J. P. Benjamin, *La.*

Fort Brown, Texas, surrendered by special agreement.

7. Georgia State Convention reassembled at Savannah.

11. Provisional Constitution of the Confederated States of America adopted in Convention at Montgomery.

13. Alabama State Convention ratified the Constitution of the Confederate States (85 *v.* 5).

16. Georgia State Convention ratified the Constitution of the Confederate States.

Provisional Congress of the Confederate States adjourned to meet again on the second Monday of May.

Arizona.—A convention held at Mesilla and an ordinance of secession passed. The C. S. Congress subsequently erected a territorial government for Arizona.

18. Supplies for Fort Pickens (Pensacola) cut off by the rebels.

19. Two New York vessels detained at Savannah by order of the Governor of Georgia were released.

The banks in Philadelphia resumed specie payments.

20. Arkansas State Convention adjourned after passing a resolution to refer the question of secession to the people.

21. Alabama State Convention adjourned *sine die.*

Louisiana State Convention ratified the Constitution of the Confederate States (101 *v.* 7).

22. Dr. Fox, of the navy, visited Major Anderson in Fort Sumter as special government messenger.

23. Georgia State Convention adjourned.

25. Col. Lamon, U. S. government messenger, had an

interview with Gov. Pickens and Gen. Beauregard.

Texas State Convention ratified the Constitution of the Confederate States.

26. South Carolina State Convention reassembled.

Texas State Convention passed an ordinance, and the Legislature approved the act, deposing Sam Houston from the executive chair in consequence of his refusal to take the new oath of allegiance to the Confederate States.

28. Vote of Louisiana on secession published: *pro* 20,448, *con* 17,296.

U. S. Senate in extra session adjourned.

30. Mississippi State Convention ratified the Constitution of the Confederate States (78 *v.* 7).

April, 1861.

1. U. S. Tariff Act went into operation.
3. Long cabinet meeting on the Fort Sumter business —great activity in the navy department.

Rebel battery on Morris Island, Charleston Harbor, fired into a schooner.

4. Legislature of Kentucky ratified the amendment to the Federal Constitution passed by Congress.

Virginia State Convention refused, by a vote 89 to 45, to submit a secession ordinance to the people.

5. South Carolina State Convention ratified the Constitution of the Confederate States (146 *v.* 16, 10 absent).
7. Gen. Beauregard notified Major Anderson that intercourse between Fort Sumter and Charleston city would no longer be permitted.

Steam transport "Atlantic" sailed from New York with troops and supplies.

8. Official notification given that supplies would be sent to Fort Sumter by force if necessary.

State department declined to recognize the C. S. commissioners.

9. U. S. steamers "Illinois" and "Baltic" sailed from New York with sealed orders.

President Davis makes a requisition for troops.

10. Floating battery at Charleston finished and mounted—large numbers of troops sent to the various fortifications.

11. Beauregard demands, by order of the Secretary of War, the unconditional surrender of Fort Sumter. Refused by Major Anderson, his own sense of honor and his obligations to the U. S. Government not permitting a compliance.

Confederate commissioners left Washington satisfied that no recognition of their government would be acceded to.

The safety of Washington provided for.

12. Bombardment of Fort Sumter—*actual commencement of the war*—began at 4.30 A.M., and continued all day and at intervals during the night.

Legislature of Pennsylvania voted $500,000 to arm the State.

Fort Pickens reinforced by U. S. troops.

13. At 7 A.M. Sumter reopened fire; at 8 the officers' quarters were fired by a rebel shell; at 10 a chance shot struck down the flag, and at noon most of the wood-work of the fort was burning, and the men rolled out 90 barrels of powder to prevent explosion, and soon after arrangements were made for the evacuation of the fort.

14. Major Anderson and his men left Fort Sumter and sailed for New York.

15. President of the United States issued his proclamation calling for 75,000 volunteers, and commanding the rebels to return to peace within 20 days. An extra session of Congress called.

The great uprising of the people of the loyal States commences. Legislatures vote men and money; banks offer loans to the Government; great public meetings are held, and proclamations, military orders, etc., become the order of the day. In the principal cities mobs visit newspaper offices and firms suspected of disloyalty and compel them to raise the stars and stripes. Union badges worn by every one.

Legislature of New York voted 30,000 men and $3,000,000 for putting down the rebellion.

16. Gov. Magoffin, of Kentucky, and Gov. Letcher, of Virginia, refused to furnish troops under the President's proclamation. Gov. Harris, of Tennessee, and Gov. Jackson, of Missouri, also refused.

Confederate States Government called for 32,600 additional troops.

17. The 6th Regiment Mass. State troops left Boston for Washington.

Virginia State Convention passed an ordinance of secession (88 *v.* 55) to take effect if ratified by the people on the 4th May next.

Gov. Letcher, of Virginia, recognized the Confederate States by proclamation.

18. U. S. steamer "Star of the West" captured by the rebels at Indianola, Tex.

U. S. Sec. of the Treasury ordered that no clearances

should be granted to vessels bound to ports south of Maryland.

Pennsylvania State Volunteers reached Washington.

Rebels obstruct the channel at Norfolk, Va., to prevent the sailing of war-vessels from that point.

Harper's Ferry Arsenal destroyed to prevent its being held by the rebels.

19. Attack on the 6th Massachusetts Regiment at Baltimore, of which two were killed and seven wounded. Eleven of the rioters killed and many wounded. Baltimore in the hands of the mob, and the mayor informed the President that no more troops could pass through the city without fighting their way.

New York Seventh left for Washington.

President of the United States issued a proclamation declaring a blockade of the ports of the seceded States, viz.: South Carolina, Georgia, Alabama, Florida, Mississippi, Louisiana, and Texas.

20. Great Union Mass Meeting in New York.

Branch mint at Charlotte, N. C., seized by the rebels.

Bridges on the Northern Central Railroad and other railroads (in Maryland) burned.

Arsenal at Liberty, Mo., seized by rebels.

Gosport (Va.) Navy Yard partially destroyed to keep it from the rebels. Property valued at $25,000,000 lost. Eleven U. S. vessels, 21,398 tons, and carrying 602 guns, scuttled. The "Cumberland" was towed out.

21. Philadelphia, Wilmington, and Baltimore Railroad taken possession of by the U. S. Government.

War sermons preached in most of the Northern churches.

22. U. S. Arsenal at Napoleon, Ark., seized by the rebels.

New York city appropriated $1,000,000 to equip volunteers, and $500,000 for their families.

23. First South Carolina regiment started for the Potomac.

Legislature of Vermont convened in extra session.

24. Fort Smith, Ark., seized by the rebels.

25. Saluria, Tex., surrendered to rebel forces.

Legislature of Vermont voted $1,000,000 to equip volunteers.

New York 7th Regiment reached Washington.

Virginia proclaimed by Governor Letcher to be a member of the Confederate States.

26. Gov. Brown, of Georgia, issued a proclamation prohibiting the payment of debts due to Northern men.

27. President's proclamation ordering the ports of Virginia and North Carolina to be blockaded.

29. Legislature of Indiana voted $500,000 to arm the State.

Legislature of Maryland repudiated secession—the Senate unanimously and the House by a vote of 53 to 15.

C. S. Congress reassemble at Montgomery.

30. Legislature of New Jersey convened in extra session; the Governor recommended the appropriation of $2,000,000 for war purposes.

Virginia State Convention passed an ordinance establishing the navy of Virginia and authorizing the banks to issue one and two dollar notes.

May, 1861.

1. Legislature of North Carolina passed a State Convention Bill.
2. New York 69th Regiment arrived in Washington.
   Ellsworth's Fire Zouaves arrived in Washington.
   Judge Campbell, of Alabama, resigned his seat in the U. S. Supreme Court.
3. Legislature of Connecticut voted $2,000,000 for public defense.
   Governor of Virginia called out the militia to defend the State from the Northerners.
   President of the United States issued a proclamation calling for 42,000 additional three-years' volunteers, 22,714 additional regulars, and 18,000 additional seamen, to be mustered into the service of the Government.
4. The Governors of Pennsylvania, Ohio, Wisconsin, Michigan, Indiana, etc., met at Cleveland, O., to devise plans for the defense of the Western States.
5. Gen. Butler, with a Union force, took possession of the Relay House, near Baltimore.
   The days of grace allowed by the President's proclamation expired.
6. Virginia admitted as a State of the Confederate States of America.
   Arkansas State Convention passed an ordinance of secession (69 *v.* 1).
   The Confederate States Congress made public the war and privateering act.
   Legislature of Tennessee passed an ordinance of secession, which was termed a Declaration of Independence, and ordered it to be voted on by the

people—passed by Senate (20 *v.* 4) and by House (46 *v.* 21).

Baltimore city militia disbanded.

7. Riot at Knoxville, Tenn., on hoisting a Union flag.

Governor of Tennessee announced a military league between that State and the Confederate States.

8. Governor of Ohio made a call for 100,000 men, to be held as a force of reserved militia.

9. C. S. Congress authorized the President to accept all the volunteers that offer.

First landing of Union troops by steamers at Baltimore.

The "Winans Steam Gun" captured on the Baltimore and Ohio Railroad.

A brigade of rebel militia encamped near St. Louis surrendered to the United States forces under Capt. Lyon.

10. The President, by proclamation, declared martial law upon the island of Key West, the Tortugas, and Santa Rosa, Fla.

Mob attack upon volunteer Home Guard in St. Louis—seven of the rioters killed.

Major-Gen. Robert E. Lee placed in command of the rebel forces in Virginia.

Officers in the Union army ordered to take the oath of allegiance.

11. Blockade of Charleston established.

Government troops again attacked by the St. Louis mob—four rioters killed, etc.

Great Union demonstration in San Francisco.

12. Renewed attempts of the rebels to destroy bridges on the railroads leading to Baltimore.

13. Anti-secession Convention of delegates from the counties of Western Virginia met at Wheeling—35 counties represented.

Union troops under Gen. Butler took possession of Federal Hill, Baltimore.

Travel through Baltimore re-established.

Blockade of the Mississippi at Cairo established.

Queen Victoria issued a proclamation enjoining neutrality in the contest between the North and South.

4. A schooner loaded with arms seized at Baltimore; arms seized in other parts of the city. Ross Winans arrested.

St. Louis and Memphis mail contract annulled, and mails stopped.

Gun-boat "Quaker City" captured ship "Argo" with $150,000 worth of tobacco.

15. Governor of Maryland issued a proclamation calling for four regiments of volunteers, in response to the President's demand.

Legislature of Massachusetts offered to loan the Government $7,000,000.

Wheeling Convention adjourned after passing resolutions in favor of the Union and recommending a division of the State of Virginia.

16. Bridges on the Baltimore and Ohio Railroad destroyed by the rebels.

Gen. Scott ordered Arlington Heights to be fortified.

Secessionists dispersed at Liberty, Mo.

17. C. S. Congress authorized the issue of $50,000,000 8 p. c. 20 years' bonds.

Secession spies arrested in Washington.

Rebels fortify Harper's Ferry.

Rebels dispersed at Potosi, Mo.

Legislature of Kentucky authorized the suspension of specie payments by the banks.

18. Rebel batteries at Sewell's Point, Va., dislodged.

This was the first offensive operation of the Government against the rebels.

Arkansas admitted as a State of the Confederate States of America.

19. Rebels at Harper's Ferry reinforced.

20. North Carolina State Convention met at Raleigh.

Seizure of telegraphic dispatches throughout the North. The object was to ascertain who were aiding the rebellion.

All mail steamships on the coasts and rivers having any connection with the rebel States stopped.

The Governor of Kentucky issued a proclamation declaring the neutrality of the State and forbidding the march of troops from either section across the State.

21. North Carolina State Convention passed unanimously an ordinance of secession.

C. S. Congress at Montgomery, Ala., adjourned to meet at Richmond, Va., on the 20th July.

Rebels establish the blockade of the Mississippi at Memphis, Tenn.

22. Ship Island fortifications destroyed to keep them from the rebels.

Flag-raising at the Post-office, Washington. Speeches of the President and cabinet officers.

24. Arlington Heights and the city of Alexandria occupied by federal troops. Col. Ellsworth shot by the rebel Jackson.

Southern mails stopped.

25. Bridges on the Alexandria and Loudon Railroad destroyed by Union troops.

26. New Orleans blockaded by the sloop of war "Brooklyn."

Alexandria placed under martial law.

27. About 100 slaves escaped from their masters and took refuge in Fortress Monroe. General Butler declared them contraband of war and legitimate prizes.
Mobile blockaded.
Brigadier-General McDowell took command at Washington.
Border States Convention assembled at Frankfort, Ky. Kentucky and Missouri only were represented.
28. Gen. Butler advanced his forces to Newport News.
Savannah blockaded.
29. President Davis reached Richmond, the new seat of the Confederate Government.
Federals advanced toward Harper's Ferry; rebels retired toward Martinsburg, Va.
30. Grafton and Williamsport, Va., evacuated by the rebels.
31. Rebel batteries at Acquia Creek, Va., silenced by Union gun-boats after an action lasting two hours.
Cavalry skirmish at Fairfax Court House, Va.

June, 1861.

1. Postal arrangements of Confederate States went into operation; United States post system suspended.
2. Battle of Philippa, Va.—rebels routed.
3. Border States Convention met at Frankfort, Ky.
Gen. Beauregard arrived at Manassas and took command of the Confederate forces.
Senator Douglas died.
6. The "Harriet Lane" engaged the Pig Point (Potomac) batteries.

Captain Ball's rebel cavalry, captured at Alexandria, sworn, and let go.

8. North Carolina State Convention ratified the C. S. Constitution.

Gen. Patterson's advance moved from Chambersburg toward Harper's Ferry.

10. Battle of Big Bethel, Va.—Union force repulsed.

Major-Gen. Banks assumed command of the Department of Annapolis.

11. Col. Wallace surprised and routed a rebel force of 800 at Romney, Va.

12. Wheeling Convention again assembled.

13. Fast day in the Confederate States, in accordance with the President's proclamation.

14. Rebels evacuated and burned Harper's Ferry, destroyed the railroad bridge, and took the armory machinery to Richmond.

Another street fight in St. Louis, in which six rebels were killed by the Union soldiers.

15. Privateer "Savannah" arrived at New York a prize of the U. S. brig "Perry."

Gen. Lyon occupied Jefferson City, Mo.

Gen. Price retreated to Booneville.

Harper's Ferry occupied by the Union forces.

16. Skirmish at Seneca Mills.

17. Wheeling Convention unanimously voted the independence of the western counties of Virginia of the rebel section of the State.

Surprise at Vienna, Va.—eight Union and six rebel soldiers killed.

Gen. Patterson crossed the Potomac at Williamsport.

18. Battle of Booneville, Mo.: rebels under Price and Jackson routed by Gen. Lyon.

Skirmish at Edward's Ferry, Va.

Affair at Cole, Mo.

19. Rebels occupied Piedmont, Va.

Wheeling Convention passed an ordinance reorganizing the State government.

20. Major-Gen. McClellan took command of the Union forces in Western Virginia.

Wheeling Convention elected Frank H. Pierpont governor of Virginia.

21. East Tennessee Union Convention met at Knoxville. On the fourth day of its session it adopted a declaration of grievances against the usurping body which voted the State out of the Union and into the Confederate States.

23. Forty-eight locomotives, valued at $400,000, belonging to the Baltimore and Ohio Railroad Company, were destroyed at Martinsburg, Va., by the rebels.

Balloon reconnoissances commenced.

24. Bank riots in Milwaukee, Wis.

Gov. Harris proclaimed Tennessee out of the Union, the vote of the people being — for separation 104,019, and against 47,238.

Large fire in Richmond, Va.

25. Virginia secession vote announced—for 128,884, and against 32,134.

Iowa voted a war loan of $600,000.

26. The President of the United States acknowledged the Wheeling government as the government of Virginia.

Skirmish at Patterson Creek, Va.: 17 rebels and one Union man killed.

27. Marshal Kane arrested in Baltimore on the charge of treason, and sent to Fort McHenry.

Engagement between U. S. gun-boats "Freeborn"

and "Pawnee" and the rebel batteries at Matthias Point, Va.: Capt. Ward, commander of the Potomac flotilla, killed.

28. Skirmish at Falls Church, Va.
Skirmish at Shooter's Hill, Va.

29. General Council of War held at Washington.

July, 1861.

1. C. S. privateer "Sumter" escaped from the "Mississippi."
C. S. privateer "Petrel" escaped from Charleston.
Late members of the Baltimore Board of Police arrested and sent to Fort McHenry.
Fight at Buckhannon, Va.
Skirmish at Falling Waters, Va.
Engagement at Haynesville, Va.
Skirmish at Farmington, Mo.

2. Engagement near Martinsburg between Patterson's (U.) and Jackson's (R.) forces: rebels defeated.
New Legislature of Virginia met and organized at Wheeling. The new government had already been recognized by the United States.

3. A rebel company (94) captured at Neosho, Mo.
Governor of Arkansas called out 10,000 men to repel invasion.

4. Anniversary of the Independence of the United States celebrated with greater feelings of patriotism than ever before throughout the Northern States.
The XXXVIIth Congress assembled in extra session. Eleven seceded States were unrepresented, except three representatives from Virginia and one sena-

tor from Tennessee. Galusha A. Grow, of Pennsylvania, elected Speaker.

Legislature of New Hampshire voted a $1,000,000 loan for the war.

Rebels seized Louisville and Nashville Railroad.

5. President's Message read in Congress: he called for 400,000 men and $400,000,000 to aid in putting down the rebellion.

Battle at Carthage, Mo. (Sigel 1,100 *v.* Jackson 4,000): rebels routed.

6. Fight at Middle York Bridge, near Buckhannon, Va.: 45 Union troops cut through an ambuscade of 200 or 300 rebels.

7. Infernal machines found in the Potomac.

Battle at Brier Forks, near Carthage, Mo. (Sigel *v.* Jackson): drawn.

8. Skirmish at Bird's Point, Mo.

Rebels routed at Bealington, Va.

Rebel camp at Florida, Mo., attacked and broken up.

Col. Taylor brought to the President a message from Jeff. Davis concerning prisoners captured as privateers.

Thomas, the "French Lady," taken in Baltimore.

9. Major-General Fremont placed in command of the Western Department.

Legislature of Virginia (Wheeling) elected John S. Carlile and Waitman T. Willey to the U. S. Senate in place of Hunter and Mason.

10. Battle at Laurel Hill (McClellan *v.* Johnson): rebels routed.

Skirmish at Monroe Station, Mo.

11. Battle at Rich Mountain, Va. (Pegram *v.* Rosecrans): rebels defeated.

U. S. Senate expel from that body Senators James

M. Mason and R. M. T. Hunter, of Virginia; Thomas L. Clingman and Thomas Bragg, of North Carolina; Louis T. Wigfall and J. W. Hemphill, of Texas; Charles B. Mitchell and William K. Sebastian, of Arkansas; and A. O. P. Nicholson, of Tennessee.

President approved the resolution of Congress remitting the duties on arms imported by States to be used in suppressing the rebellion.

12. Union troops under McClellan took possession of Beverly, Va.: Col. Pegram surrendered with his entire force.

Skirmish at Newport News, Va.

Skirmish at Barboursville, Va.

13. Battle of Carrickford, Va. (Morris *v.* Garnett): rebels defeated and Gen. Garnett killed. Rebel power in Western Virginia broken.

U. S. House of Representatives expelled John B. Clark, member from Missouri, by a vote 94 *v.* 45.

15. Union army, 40,000 strong, under McDowell, moved from encampments in and around Washington and Arlington Heights toward Fairfax Court House, Va.

Skirmish at Bunker Hill, Va.: rebels routed.

16. Rebel pickets driven beyond Fairfax Court House, Va.

Battle at Barboursville, Va.: rebels defeated.

Tighlman, a negro, killed three of the rebel prize crew on the schooner "S. J. Waring," and brought the vessel into New York.

Skirmish at Millville, Mo.

17. Union army continued their march toward Fairfax Court House.

Skirmish at Fulton, Mo.

18. FIRST BATTLE OF BULL RUN: an engagement took place at Blackford's Ford, Bull Run, between Union troops under Gen. Tyler and the rebels under Beauregard. Gen. Tyler fell back to Centreville.
19. Gen. Banks superseded Gen. Patterson in command on the Potomac.
20. C. S. Congress met at Richmond.

Union army moved from Fairfax Court House and vicinity toward Manassas Junction.

The rebels under Gen. H. A. Wise fled from the valley of the Big Kanawha on the approach of the Union troops.

21. SECOND BATTLE OF BULL RUN (McDowell *v.* Beauregard): conflict lasted 10 hours, when a panic seized the Union forces, which fled in disorder to Washington. The loss was as follows:

Union....481 killed....1,011 wounded...1,216 missing=2,698
Rebel....630 " ....2,235 " ... 150 " =3,015

—The numbers engaged were—Union 40,000 *v.* rebel 47,000, the latter of which were reinforced during the battle by 20,000 or 25,000.

22. Gens. McDowell and Mansfield superseded in command of the Army of the Potomac by Gen. McClellan. Army disorganized, and the three months' men return home.

State Convention of Missouri met at Jefferson City.

25. Governor of New York called for 25,000 additional troops.

Skirmish at Harrisonville, Va.

Gen. McClellan takes command of the Army of the Potomac.

26. Union troops drove out the rebels and occupied Forsyth, Mo.

27. Return of the 69th and other regiments to New York.
28. Gen. Banks at Harper's Ferry withdrew his troops to the Maryland side of the Potomac.
29. Robert Toombs, of Georgia, resigned his position as C. S. Secretary of State, and was succeeded by Robert M. T. Hunter, of Virginia.
30. Missouri State Convention declared vacant the offices of Governor, Lieutenant-Governor, and Secretary of State, by a vote of 56 to 25. The seats of the members of the Legislature were also declared vacant. The State officers and a majority of the Legislature were secessionists.
31. Missouri State Convention elected Hamilton R. Gamble Governor, Willard P. Hall Lieutenant-Governor, and Mordecai Oliver Secretary of State —all Union men.

August, 1861.

1. Gen. McClellan began the reorganization of the Army of the Potomac.

   Rebels left Harper's Ferry and fell back on Leesburg.

   C. S. privateer "Petrel" sunk by the "St. Lawrence" —crew captured.
2. War-Tax and Tariff bill passed Congress—500,000 men and $500,000,000 to be raised.

   Battle of Dug Spring, Mo. (Lyon *v.* McCulloch.)

   Fort Fillmore, New Mexico, traitorously surrendered, with 750 men, by Major Lynde.

   Rebel vessels and stores destroyed in Pocomoke Sound.

3. U. S. blockading fleet threw a few shells into Galveston, Tex.; foreign consuls protest, etc.
4. Skirmish at Point of Rocks, Va.
   Rebels routed at Athens, Mo.
6. U. S. Congress in extra session adjourned *sine die.*
7. Hampton, Va., burned by the rebels.
   C. S. privateer "York" burned by the gun-boat "Union."
8. Rebels routed at Lovettsville, Va.
   Office of the *Democratic Standard*, a secession paper, at Concord, N. H., cleaned out by a mob, and the materials burned in the street.
9. Rebels attacked and routed at Potosi, Mo.
10. Battle of Wilson's Creek, about 12 miles from Springfield, Mo. (Lyon *v.* McCulloch and Price): Union force 5,200, and rebel 15,000—rebels, after six hours' fighting, repulsed. Gen. Lyon killed. During the night the Union forces fell back to Springfield, and thence to Rolla. Rebels too much disabled to follow. Union loss, 263 killed and 721 wounded; rebel loss, 421 killed and 1,300 wounded.
11. Rebel company captured at Georgetown, Mo.
12. Arrest of Hon. C. J. Faulkner, late U. S. Minister to France.
    Office of the Bangor (Me.) *Democrat*, a secession paper, entirely destroyed by a mob.
13. Rebels driven from Grafton, Va., and the place occupied by Union troops—21 rebels killed.
    Skirmish at Matthias Point, Va.
14. Martial law was declared in St. Louis by Major-Gen. Fremont.
    Mutiny in the 79th New York Regiment at Washington.

15. President Davis ordered all Northern men to leave the Confederacy within 40 days.

16. President Lincoln declared by proclamation the States of Virginia, North Carolina, Tennessee, and Arkansas in insurrection, and ordered all commercial intercourse between the North and seceded States to cease.

Rebel camp at Fredericktown, Md., attacked, and 12 of the enemy taken prisoners.

Several newspapers in New York presented by the grand jury for hostility to the Government.

18. Gen. Wool took command of Fortress Monroe.

Skirmishes at Charleston, Mo.

Sentinel office at Easton, Pa., destroyed by a mob—cause, secession proclivities.

19. U. S. Sec. of War issued an order calling upon governors of States to send immediately to Washington all regiments and parts of regiments within their respective jurisdictions.

U. S. Sec. of State ordered that all persons leaving or entering the United States shall be possessed of a passport.

Editor of the *Essex County* (Mass.) *Democrat* was tarred and feathered for rebel sentiments.

Offices of the *Jeffersonian*, Westchester, Pa., and of the *People's Friend*, Covington, Ind., cleaned out by mobs—both secession.

20. Skirmish at Hawk's Nest, in the Kanawha Valley, Va.: 4,000 rebels attacked the barricades of the 11th Ohio Regiment, and were driven back with the loss of 50 killed.

Attack on Charleston, Mo., and rout of 1,200 rebels.

Wheeling Convention passed an ordinance, erecting a new State to be called "Kanawha," by a vote of 50 to 28. The boundary as fixed included the counties of—Logan, Wyoming, Raleigh, Fayette, Nicholas, Webster, Randolph, Tucker, Preston, Monongahela, Marion, Taylor, Barbour, Upshur, Harrison, Lewis, Braxton, Clay, Kanawha, Boone, Wayne, Cabell, Putnam, Mason, Jackson, Roan, Calhoun, Wirt, Gilmer, Ritchie, Wood, Pleasants, Tyler, Doddridge, Wetzel, Marshall, Ohio, Brooke, and Hancock. Other adjoining counties might be admitted, if acceded to by a majority of the voters.

21. Wheeling Convention adjourned *sine die.*

Skirmish at Cross Lanes, Va.

23. A large portion of the Cherokee Indians seceded and joined the Confederates.

24. Offices of the Bridgeport (Ct.) *Farmer* and of the Cumberland (Md.) *Alleghanian* (secession papers) destroyed by mobs.

Mayor Berrett, of Washington, D. C., arrested on charge of treason, and conveyed to Fort Lafayette.

Gov. Gamble, of Missouri, issued a proclamation calling for 42,000 troops to assist in driving the rebels from the State.

Transmission of secession journals through the mails prohibited.

26. Seventh Ohio Regiment, while breakfasting at Summersville, Va., surprised and surrounded by a force of rebels under Floyd, but fought themselves through with a comparatively small loss.

Naval and military expedition sailed from Fortress Monroe against the forts at Hatteras Inlet.

28. Bombardment and capture of forts Clark and Hatteras on the coast of North Carolina; rebel loss—765 prisoners, 1,000 stand of arms, two vessels loaded with cotton and coffee, and a large amount

of ammunition and stores. Union commanders: Stringham of the navy, and Butler of the army.

29. Lexington, Mo., attacked by 2,000 rebels. The place was defended by 250 men, who successfully beat off their assailants.

Twenty-three rebels captured at Greytown, Mo.

30. Fort Morgan, at Okracoke, abandoned by the rebels.

31. Major-Gen. Fremont issued a proclamation declaring martial law throughout Missouri, and also declaring that the property of rebels should be confiscated, their slaves freed, and themselves, if found guilty by court-martial, shot.

September, 1861.

1. Fight at Boone Court House, Va.; rebels routed and village burned.

Fight at Bennett's Mills, Mo.

2. Sec. of the Treasury issued an appeal to the people for a national loan.

Legislature of Kentucky met; Senate 27 Union and 11 secession; House 76 Union and 24 secession

Floating dock at Pensacola, Fla., burned.

3. Massacre on Hannibal and St. Joseph Railroad; the rebels having burned the Platte Bridge, the train fell into the river—17 lives lost.

5. Columbus, Ky., occupied by the C. S. forces.

6. Paducah, Ky., occupied by the U. S. forces.

9. Union prisoners (156) taken at Bull Run, sent from Richmond to Castle Pinckney, Charleston Harbor.

10. Battle of Carnifex Ferry, Va. Rosecrans defeated

the rebels under Floyd and captured large quantities of arms, ammunition, equipage, stores, etc.

Rebel batteries at Lucas Bend, Ky. (Mississippi River), attacked by Union gun-boats and silenced; 68 rebels killed.

Colors of the New York 79th Regiment restored.

11. Kentucky Legislature passed a resolution ordering the C. S. troops to leave the State.

President Lincoln, in a letter to Gen. Fremont, directs him to modify the confiscation clause of his proclamation.

A number of fine vessels captured by the Union fleet at Hatteras Inlet.

Skirmish at Lewinsville, Va.; rebels defeated.

Skirmish at Elk Water, Va.; Union troops victorious.

Skirmish at Stewart's Mill, Va.

12. Col. John A. Washington (rebel), former proprietor of Mount Vernon, killed near Elk Water, Va., while reconnoitering.

Mayor Berrett, of Washington, took the oath and was released from Fort Lafayette.

The provost-marshal of St. Louis issued a proclamation manumitting two slaves, the property of a secessionist.

Battle of Cheat Mountain, Va.; rebels defeated.

13. Booneville, Mo., attacked by rebels, who were repulsed by the Home Guard stationed there.

Thirteen members of the Maryland Legislature, two editors of secession newspapers, one member of Congress, and the gubernatorial candidate of the secession party arrested in Baltimore.

C. S. privateer "Judith" destroyed at Pensacola,

Fla., by a boat expedition from the U. S. ship "Colorado."

14. Skirmish near Shepherdstown, Va.

15. Skirmish near Darnestown, Va.; rebels repulsed.

16. Ship Island evacuated by the C. S. forces and occupied by Union troops.

Camp Talbot, Mo., captured by Union troops.

Rebels under Gen. Price commenced the bombardment of Lexington, Mo.

17. Skirmish at Blue Mills Landing, Mo. · Union troops repulsed.

Bridge on the Ohio and Mississippi Railroad, near Huron, broke through while a train of cars with the Illinois 19th Regiment was passing over; 26 were killed and 112 wounded.

Legislature of Maryland was to have met, but on account of the recent arrest of its secession members there was no quorum.

Skirmish at Mariatown, Mo.

18. Members (18), Speaker, and clerk of the Maryland Legislature arrested at Frederick and sent to Fort McHenry.

Banks of New Orleans suspended specie payments.

Skirmish near Columbus and Barboursville, Kentucky.

19. Ex-Gov. Morehead and others in Louisville arrested for treason.

20. Surrender of Col. Mulligan at Lexington, Mo., after four days' struggle with 2,500 men against 26,000 rebels under Gen. Price.

Skirmish near Tuscumbia, Mo.

21. John C. Breckinridge fled from Frankfort, Ky., and openly joined the rebels.

Severe fight at Papinsville, Mo., resulting in the defeat of the rebels and capture of arms, stores, etc., by the Union forces.

22. Skirmish at Ellicott's Mills, Ky.

24. Count de Paris and Duc de Chartres entered the U. S. service as aids to Gen. McClellan.

Grand review of troops at Washington.

Romney, Va., stormed and captured by U. S. troops.

25. Gen. Prentiss took command of the Union forces at St. Joseph.

Skirmish near Chapmansville, Va.

26. National Fast, observed in accordance with President Lincoln's recommendation.

Second action at Lucas Bend, Ky.; rebel loss four killed and five prisoners.

27. Gen. Fremont takes the field against the rebels· left St. Louis with 13,000 men.

28. Rebel forces fall back from their positions before Washington, and the U. S. troops again occupied Munson's and Upton's hills and Falls Church, Va.

29. Two advance bodies of the Union troops came into collision by mistaking each other for the enemy, near Falls Church, and before the error was discovered 15 were killed and 30 or 40 wounded.

October, 1861.

1. Rebel camp at Charleston, Mo., broken up by Union troops.

U. S. transport "Fanny" captured by two rebel steamers between Hatteras Inlet and Chicamacomico.

2. Rebels defeated at Chapmansville, Va.

3. Battle at Greenbrier, Va.; rebels defeated after an

hour's fighting, and a large number of cattle and horses taken by the U. S. troops.

Ex-Street Commissioner of New York, Gustavus W. Smith, appointed a brig.-general in the rebel army.

Rebels evacuated Lexington, Mo.

Skirmish at Buffalo Hill, Ky.; Union loss 10 killed and 10 wounded; rebel loss 52 killed, etc.

5. Unsuccessful efforts of the rebels to retake the Hatteras Inlet forts.

Gen. Robert Anderson took command of the Union forces in Kentucky.

6. Skirmish at Flemington, Ky.; Home Guards defeated the rebels.

7. Gen. W. F. Sherman, relieved.

Gen. Robert Anderson relieved of his command in Kentucky, his health not permitting him to enter on active service.

Gen. Fremont and his army leave Jefferson City, Mo., in pursuit of the rebels under Gen. Price.

9. Rebels attack Santa Rosa Island, Fla., and are repulsed by regulars and Wilson's Zouaves.

Advance of the Union lines beyond the Potomac; Lewinsville occupied.

Charter election in Baltimore—no disturbance by the secessionists.

All the banks in Pittsburg, Pa., resumed specie payments.

10. Further advances of the Union troops into Virginia.

11. Rebel steamer "Nashville" escaped from Charleston Harbor.

Missouri State Convention met.

Marshal Kane sent to Fort Lafayette.

12. Attack by a rebel gun-boat fleet and five ships from New Orleans on the Union blockading squadron,

at the head of the Mississippi passes. The rebel vessels were beaten off and their iron-clad "turtle" considerably damaged.

Rebels advanced in force toward Prospect Hill, but retired on finding Gen. McCall ready for battle.

13. Skirmishing at Beckwith and Tavern Creek, Mo.

14. Sec. Seward issued a circular to governors of States, advising sea-coast and lake defenses.

Linn Creek, Mo., captured by U. S. troops, and a company of rebel troops taken prisoners.

15. Jeff. Thompson captured 50 Union troops at Potosi, Mo.

Three steamers dispatched from New York after the "Nashville."

Defeat of the rebels at Frederick, Mo.

16. Recapture of Lexington, Mo., by a small Union force under Major White, the main body of the rebels having previously evacuated the city.

Rebels routed at Bolivar, near Harper's Ferry

Sharp skirmish at Ironton, Mo.

Battle at Pilot Knob, Mo.; rebels routed.

17. Rebel army retired from Halifax Court House and also from Leesburg, Va.

18. Pacific Telegraph Line completed to Great Salt Lake City. Brigham Young, the Mormon chief, sent a congratulatory dispatch to President Lincoln.

19. Skirmish at Big Hurricane Creek, Carroll Co., Mo.

21. Union fleet, consisting of twenty steamers, sailed from Annapolis, Md., bound south.

Battle of Ball's Bluff. Part of Gen. Stone's division crossed the Potomac at Ball's Bluff, and after severe fighting, during which Col. Baker was killed, was driven back with great loss by the enemy;

killed, 223, wounded 165, wounded among prisoners 100, prisoners not wounded 421, total 918. The rebel loss is supposed to have been about 500 killed and wounded.

Battle of Wild Cat, Ky.; Zollicoffer (rebel) defeated by Shoepf (Union).

Rebels under Jeff. Thompson defeated at Fredericktown, Mo.

22\. Office of the *Democrat* (secession), at Terre Haute, Ind., destroyed by a portion of the 43d Indiana Regiment.

Rebel camp at Buffalo Mills, Mo., broken up.

The rebel batteries on the Potomac River, below Washington, extended from Cockpit Point to Matthias Point, a distance of 20 miles.

23\. Writ of habeas corpus suspended in the District of Columbia, in all cases relating to the military.

Skirmish at West Liberty, Mo.

24\. Western section of Pacific Telegraph Line connected with the eastern section of Great Salt Lake City, thus connecting the wires between the Atlantic and Pacific coasts.

26\. Rebels routed by the Union troops at Romney, Va., retreated to Winchester.

Gallant charge of Major Zagonyi, of Fremont's Body Guard, with 160 men, through a rebel force 2,000 strong, at Springfield, Mo.; rebels signally defeated and many of them killed.

28\. A rebel transportation train captured by Gen. Lane near Butler, Mo.

Battle at Cromwell, Ky.; rebels lost two killed and five wounded.

Battle at Saratoga, Ky.: Union loss three wounded; rebel loss 13 killed, 17 wounded, and 44 prisoners.

29. The great naval and military expedition, destined to operate off the Southern coast, sailed from Hampton Roads at 6 A.M.—naval under Com. Dupont and military under Gen. T. W. Sherman. The expedition was composed of the following vessels: three war steamers, six sail war-vessels, 26 steam gun-boats, four steam ferry-boats, 30 steam transports, and six sail transports. About 27,000 troops accompanied the expedition.

Rebels routed at Woodbury, Ky., with a loss of 50 killed and a large number wounded.

30. All the State prisoners (148) in Fort Lafayette were removed to Fort Warren, Boston Harbor.

31. Rebels attacked the Union camp at Morgantown, Ky., but were repulsed with considerable loss.

November, 1861.

1. Lieut.-Gen. Winfield Scott, Commander of the United States Army, was placed by the President on the retired list of army officers, without reduction of his pay, subsistence, or allowances.

Major-Gen. George B. McClellan assumed command of the armies of the United States in place of Gen. Scott.

Rebels under Floyd attempted to capture Rosecrans' army at Gauley Bridge, Va., but failed, and Floyd only saved himself by a precipitate flight.

A violent storm overtook the great Union naval and military expedition off the coast of North Carolina, and effected considerable damage.

2. Major-Gen. Fremont removed from the command of the Western armies.

Rebel steamer "Bermuda" runs the blockade off Savannah.

Rebels routed near Leavenworth, Kansas.

Spirited engagement at Platte City, Mo.

Prestonburg, Ky., taken by Union forces.

3. Rising of the Union men of East Tennessee, who in the following few days burn and break down several important railroad bridges.

4. Twenty-five vessels of the great Southern naval and military expedition, including the flag-ship "Wabash," anchored off Port Royal Harbor, South Carolina.

Houston, Mo., taken possession of by federal forces, who captured a large amount of rebel property, a number of rebel soldiers and secessionists, and a large mail for the rebel army.

5. Skirmish at Boston, Ky.

6. A Union force of 3,500 men, under Gen. Grant, left Cairo, Ill., in four steamers and two gun-boats, and landed three miles above Columbus, Ky.

7. Great naval fight off Hilton Head, Port Royal entrance; forts Walker and Beauregard bombarded and captured by the Union forces.

8. Battle of Belmont, Mo., between the expedition under Grant and the rebels. The Union men retired before large rebel reinforcements from Columbus, Ky., their retreat being covered by the gun-boats. Great slaughter on both sides; Union loss—killed 84, wounded 288, and missing and prisoners 235—total 607; rebel loss—killed 261, wounded 427, and prisoners 278—total 966.

Rebels captured 120 Union troops at Little Santa Fe, Mo.

Capture of the rebel commissioners Slidell and Mason on the British mail steamer "Trent" by the U. S. war sloop "San Jacinto."

Com. Dupont, of the naval expedition, sent a force up Port Royal Harbor to examine the town of Beaufort; the place was found to be deserted.

9. Major-Gen. H. W. Halleck assigned to the command of the Department of the West, and Gen. Don Carlos Buel to the Department of Kentucky.

10. Sharp skirmish in the Kanawha Valley, Va.: rebels pursued 25 miles.

Union forces at Guyandotte, Va., on the Ohio River, having been betrayed and a number of them murdered by the rebel inhabitants of the town, the place was fired and about two thirds of the houses destroyed.

11. Skirmish near Kansas City, Mo.

Major-Gen. Halleck assumed command of the Department of the West *vice* Fremont.

Battle of Piketon, Ky.: Union loss one killed and 22 wounded; rebel loss 32 killed.

12. Reconnoissance in force from Alexandria to the Occoquan River; no rebels discovered.

14. Cumberland River railroad bridge burned by the Union men of East Tennessee.

15. U. S. steamer "San Jacinto," Capt. Wilkes, arrived in Hampton Roads, having on board Mason and Slidell, the rebel commissioners sent by the C. S. Government to negotiate treaties with the European powers.

16. A train of 50 wagons and 500 head of cattle captured by the rebels in Cass Co., Mo.

A federal foraging party of 52 men captured by rebel cavalry near Falls Church, Va.

17. Wagons and cattle captured by the rebels in Cass

County, Mo., recaptured by a party of Union troops.

18. Union cavalry captured 150 rebels near Warrensburg, Mo.

Rebels in Accomac and Northampton counties, Va., disbanded, and Union troops took possession of the peninsula.

C. S. Congress convened at Richmond.

Convention of delegates representing 42 counties of North Carolina met at Hatteras, declared against the action of the State Convention held at Raleigh, 20th May, and appointed Marble Nash Taylor Provisional Governor of North Carolina, with power to fill all official vacancies by temporary appointments. Election of senators and representatives to U. S. Congress ordered.

19. Missouri State Convention (rebel) passed an ordinance of secession.

Warsaw, Mo., burned by the rebels.

Expedition of the gun-boat "Conestoga" up the Tennessee River; she discovered two batteries, and succeeded in dislodging the rebels.

20. Gen. Floyd evacuates his camps near Gauley River, Va., and makes a hasty retreat, burning 300 tents and destroying a large amount of equipage.

A fleet of 30 old whalers loaded with stones sailed from New Bedford and New London, bound South, for the purpose of being sunk in the channels at the entrance of some of the Southern ports.

Grand review of 60,000 troops by Gen. McClellan.

22. Fort Pickens, Florida, opened fire on the rebel batteries at Pensacola, which was answered by forts Barrancas and McRae.

23. The firing between Fort Pickens and the rebel batteries was continued. Fort McRae effectually silenced; Fort Barrancas and the Navy Yard materially damaged, and the town of Warrington mostly burned. Fort Pickens had one gun disabled. The war vessels "Niagara" and "Richmond" took part in the engagement on the first day, but were prevented on the second on account of the lowness of the water.

24. Mason and Slidell placed in Fort Warren, Boston Harbor.

Tybee Island, mouth of Savannah River, occupied by federal forces.

Skirmish at Lancaster, Mo.

25. While collecting the shot and shell fired by the enemy at Fort Pickens, a shell burst and killed five and wounded seven of our soldiers.

26. Springfield, Mo., again occupied by the rebels under Ben McCulloch.

Reinforcements left New York for Port Royal.

Skirmish near Vienna, Va.: rebel success.

27. Action at Black Walnut Creek, Mo.

28. Thanksgiving Day duly observed throughout the loyal States.

29. Skirmish near Newmarket, Va.

Train on the Platte County (Mo.) Railroad seized on its arrival at Weston by guerrillas under the rebel Gordon.

December, 1861.

2. First regular session of the XXXVIIth Congress commenced at Washington.

Loyal Legislature of Virginia met at Wheeling.

Naval skirmish at Newport News.

3. H. C. Burnett, a representative in Congress from Kentucky, and John W. Reed, a representative from Missouri, expelled from the House of Representatives, being traitors to their country.

Skirmish at Salem, Mo.

Steamship "Constitution," with the Massachusetts 26th and Connecticut 9th, being the advance of Gen. Butler's expedition, arrived at Ship Island and landed troops on the Mississippi coast.

Fortification at Bolivar Point, Galveston Harbor, Tex., destroyed by the U. S. frigate "Santee."

4. John C. Breckinridge, of Kentucky, declared a traitor, and expelled from the U. S. Senate by a unanimous vote.

5. Major-Gen. Halleck ordered the arrest of every man found in arms against the Union in Missouri. Those found guilty of aiding the rebels to be shot.

Reports of the Secretaries of War and the Navy show that there were in the service of the U. S. Government 682,971 men, viz., volunteers 640,637, regular army 20,334, and seamen and marines 22,000.

6. Riot at Nashville, Tenn., caused by drafting for soldiers to supply the rebel army.

Occupation of Beaufort, S. C., by U. S. forces.

7. Skirmish near Dam No. 5 on the Potomac.

Company of rebels captured at Glasgow, Mo.

9. U. S. Congress passed measures to effect an exchange of prisoners.

Confiscation (Gurley's) Bill introduced to Congress.

Garrett Davis elected senator from Kentucky in place of the traitor Breckinridge.

C. S. Congress passed a bill admitting Kentucky to the Confederacy.

Detachment of another stone fleet, composed of seven vessels, left New Bedford for a Southern port.

10. Shelling of Free Stone Point by Union gun-boats.

11. Great fire in Charleston, S. C.: half of the city burned.

All the islands adjacent to Port Royal occupied by Union forces, and the work of cotton-picking on the plantations commenced.

13. First military execution in the Union army: a deserter named Johnson shot.

Battle at Camp Alleghany (Milroy *v.* Johnson): rebels ran away during the night.

Papinsville, Mo., burned by the Union troops; also, the town of Butler, Bates Co., Mo.

15. News from England of the feeling concerning the capture of Mason and Slidell: apprehensions of a war with Great Britain.

Picket fight at Point of Rocks, Va.

16. Platte City, Mo., fired by the rebels, and the principal buildings burned.

17. Battle at Munfordsville, on Green River, Ky.: rebel loss, 33 killed and 50 wounded; Union loss, 10 killed and 17 wounded.

Seven vessels loaded with stone sunk at the entrance of Savannah Harbor.

18. Gen. Pope's forces surprised the enemy's camps near Shawnee Mound and at Milford, Mo., and succeeded in capturing many prisoners and large amounts of stores, ammunition, etc. About 2,500 prisoners were taken in three days.

20. Battle of Drainesville, Va., in which the Union

troops under Gen. McCall signally defeated the rebels.

Rebels destroyed about 100 miles of the North Missouri Railroad—from Hudson to Warrentown. All the bridges, wood-piles, water-tanks, ties, rails, and telegraph poles burned.

21. All the Charleston insurance companies, except one, broke down and went into liquidation.

Entrance to Charleston Harbor effectually closed by sinking 17 stone vessels across the channel.

22. Surprise of the Union forces near Newmarket Bridge, Va.

23. Thirteen rebel prisoners taken by Gen. Pope arrive at St. Louis.

24. Bill to assess and increase the duties on tea, coffee, sugar, and molasses passed Congress.

War Department issued orders suspending the enlistment of cavalry soldiers.

25. Christmas Day observed in all the Union camps, such cheer being distributed to the soldiers as was within reach.

26. Hon. Alfred Ely returned to Washington from Richmond, where he had been confined as a prisoner since the battle of Bull Run. He was exchanged for Hon. Charles J. Faulkner, late U. S. Minister to France.

28. Diplomatic correspondence in relation to the Mason-Slidell affair given to the public. The United States Government acceded to the demands of England.

Affair at Mt. Sion, Mo.: rebels (900) under Dorsey beaten and dispersed by Union troops (500) under Prentiss.

29. Skirmish in Adair Co , Ky.

30. Banks of New York, Philadelphia, Albany, and Boston suspended specie payments.

Slidell and Mason delivered to the British Minister.

31. The army of the United States at the close of the year was made up as follows:

Volunteers	640,637
Regulars	20,334
Total	660,971

The effective force of the navy, not including vessels on the stocks or unfit for service, was as follows:

Classes.	Sailing Vessels.	No. of Guns.	Steam Vessels.	No. of Guns.
Frigates	6	300	6	222
Sloops	17	342	37	326
Brigs	2	12	—	—
Small side-wheel	—	—	16	56
Iron-clad	—	—	3	18
Gun-boats (new)	—	—	23	92
Gun-boats (purchased)	—	—	79	342
Sloops (purchased)	13	52	—	—
Barks (purchased)	18	28	—	—
Brigs (purchased)	2	4	—	—
Schooners (purchased)	24	49	—	—
Total	82	837	164	1,055

Total: vessels 246 and guns 1,892. Seamen and marines, 22,000.

January, 1862.

1. Mason and Slidell were transferred from Fort Warren to the British gun-boat "Rinaldo" at Provincetown, Mass., bound for England.

Fort Pickens, Fla., opened fire on the rebel batteries at Pensacola. Firing interchanged through the whole day. A breach was made in Fort Barrancas and the town of Warrington set on fire.

2. Battle on Port Royal Island, S. C.: a number of rebel batteries destroyed, and the rebels driven from the island.

Fight between the Union gun-boats "Yankee" and "Anacostia," of the Potomac flotilla, and the rebel batteries at Cockpit Point.

Steamer "Ella Warley" ran the blockade into Charleston, S. C.

3. Union troops took possession of Big Bethel, Va., the rebels having evacuated the place.

4. Huttonsville, Va., attacked by the Union troops, and the rebel stores deposited there destroyed.

Fight at Bath, Va.: Union troops fell back on Hancock, Md.

5. Rebels on opposite side of the Potomac shelled Hancock, Md., but were driven off by the Union artillery.

6. Gen. Milroy attacked and routed a party of 400 rebels in Tucker Co., Va.

Rebel encampment of 1,000 men under Poindexter, in Howard Co., Mo., attacked and completely routed by 500 Union cavalry under Major Hubbard.

7. Gov. Morehead, of Kentucky, released from Fort Warren.

Gun-boat reconnoissance to within two miles of Columbus, Ky.

Paintville, Ky., captured from the rebels under Humphrey Marshall by the Unionists under Gen. Garfield.

Rebels at Romney, Va., surprised and routed.

8. Rebels, 2,000 strong, at Blue's Gap, Va., routed by

a detachment of Union forces under Col. Duming, who captured two cannons and all their equipage.

Rebels in Randolph Co., Mo., routed.

9. Slight skirmish at Pohick Run, Va.

10. Gen. Garfield overtaking Humphrey Marshall's forces at the forks of Middle Creek, near Prestonburg, Ky., a fight ensued, which resulted in the total defeat of the rebels.

Naval and military expedition left Cairo, bound down the Mississippi.

Union troops evacuated Romney, Va.

Waldo P. Johnson and Trusten Polk, both of Missouri, expelled from the United States Senate as traitors.

11. Gun-boat action near Columbus, Ky.

Bridges of the Louisville and Nashville Railroad burned by the rebels.

12. Sloop of war "Pensacola" run past the rebel batteries on the Potomac.

Expedition consisting of 125 vessels left Fortress Monroe bound south. The expedition took about 15,000 troops in three brigades under Gen. A. E. Burnside. The fleet was commanded by Com. L. M. Goldsborough, U. S. Navy.

13. Simon Cameron, U. S. Sec. of War, resigned. Edwin M. Stanton, of Pennsylvania, appointed his successor. Cameron nominated U. S. Minister to Russia *vice* C. M. Clay resigned.

14. Gun-boat reconnoissance to Columbus, Ky.

15. Rebel lightship off Wilmington, N. C., burned by the Union blockading force.

16. Ohio Legislature passed a law authorizing the banks of the State to suspend specie payments.

17. The advance of Burnside's Expedition arrived at

Hatteras Inlet, N. C., after meeting with heavy gales.

Cedar Keys, Fla., captured by the Union forces.

18. Reconnoissance up the Tennessee River by the U. S. gun-boat "Conestoga."

Death of ex-President John Tyler, at Richmond Va.

19. Battle of Mill Spring, Ky. A rebel force 10,000 strong under Gens. G. B. Crittenden and Felix K. Zollicoffer attacked the Union forces (four regiments) under Gen. Thomas. The latter were dreadfully cut up, but after the first and severest engagement they were reinforced by nine regiments and several batteries, and completely routed their antagonists, who were driven back to their intrenchments on the Cumberland River, which they recrossed during the night and retreated in confusion. Gen. Zollicoffer was killed during the fight. The Unionists captured 10 cannon, 100 wagons, 1,200 horses, 1,000 muskets, several boxes of arms, and large quantities of ammunition and subsistence stores, together with a number of boats. Rebel loss: 192 killed, 68 wounded, and 89 prison ers; Union loss: 39 killed and 207 wounded.

Rebel schooner "Lizzie Weston" captured.

20. Order issued for the appointment of commissioners to visit Richmond to provide for the welfare of the Union troops imprisoned at that place.

Rebel schooner "Wilder" captured in Mobile Bay.

21. Gen. McClernand's expedition returned to Cairo from reconnoitering in the vicinity of Columbus, Ky.

22. A convention at Great Salt Lake City, Utah Ter., adopted a State Constitution to be submitted to

Congress, with a request to be admitted into the Union. The name of the new State to be Deseret.

23. A second fleet of stone-laden vessels sunk in Charleston Harbor.

Rebel steamer "Calhoun" captured off the South-West Pass, mouth of the Mississippi.

24. Two rebel vessels grounded in an attempt to run the blockade at the mouth of the Mississippi. They were burned.

Twelve rebel officers and 68 privates captured at Bloomfield, Mo.

26. Anniversary of the secession of Louisiana: the day celebrated in New Orleans.

Reconnoissance toward Munfordsville, Ky.

Most of the vessels of the Burnside Expedition passed through Hatteras Inlet into Pamlico Sound.

27. Bishop Ames and Hon. Hamilton Fish appointed commissioners to visit Richmond, and look to the comfort of the Union prisoners.

28. Gun-boat reconnoissance in the neighborhood of Fort Pulaski, below Savannah, Ga. Engagement between Union and rebel boats—the latter under Com. Tatnall.

29. A small Union force surrounded a house near Occoquan River, Va., where nine Texan rangers were stationed, and in the skirmish which ensued killed the whole nest.

30. The "Monitor" launched.

The answer of Lord Russell to the dispatch of Sec. Seward surrendering Mason and Slidell arrived in this country.

31. All the saltpetre in the rebel States ordered to be seized for the government, and fifty cents a pound allowed therefor.

February, 1862.

1. Skirmish near Bowling Green, Ky.
2. Cavalry skirmish in Morgan Co., Tenn.
3. The privateersmen confined in the city jails as pirates having been declared prisoners of war, were removed to Fort Lafayette.

Rebel steamer "Nashville" ordered to leave Southampton (Eng.) Harbor; the U. S. gun-boat "Tuscarora" starting in pursuit was stopped by the British frigate "Shannon."

4. Brisk skirmish on the Potomac near Occoquan, Va.

Discussion in the rebel House of Delegates of Virginia on the subject of enrolling free negroes.

Address published by the rebel commanders appealing to the men whose terms of enlistment were about to expire to rejoin the army.

5. Jesse D. Bright, of Indiana, expelled from the U. S. Senate by a vote of 32 to 14.

Skirmish near Beaufort, S. C.

Gen. Thos. F. Meagher took command of the Irish Brigade in McClellan's army.

British schooner "Mars" captured off Florida.

6. Fort Henry, on the Tennessee River, taken by the Union Western gun-boat fleet under Com. A. H. Foote. Gen. Lloyd Tilghman and his staff taken prisoners. The fort mounted 17 guns. Union loss: 17 killed and 31 wounded. Rebel loss: 19 killed and 8 wounded.
7. Cavalry skirmish near Fairfax C. H., Va.

Harper's Ferry shelled by the Union batteries and a large number of buildings destroyed and burned.

Romney, Va., occupied by Union troops under Gen. Lander.

Two rebel transports on the Tennessee River destroyed.

7 and 8. Battle of Roanoke Island: the island with all its fortifications captured. Six batteries mounting 46 guns, 3,000 small-arms, and large quantities of supplies fell into the hands of Gen. Burnside. Union loss: 50 killed and 222 wounded. Rebel loss: 13 killed, 39 wounded, and 2,527 prisoners.

8. Rebel boats, "Sallie Wood" and "Muscle," captured at Chickasaw, Miss.

Three rebel steamboats burned at Florence, la.

Gen. Hunter declared martial law throughout the State of Kansas.

Bridge of the Louisville, Clarkesville and Memphis railroads over the Tennessee burned by Union forces.

Expedition (13 gun-boats) sent up the Pasquotank River toward Elizabeth City, N. C., whither the rebel gun-boats had fled after the battle of Roanoke Island.

9. Brig.-Gen. C. P. Stone arrested and sent to Fort Lafayette. The charges against him related principally to the Ball's Bluff disaster.

10. Union gun-boats returned from the expedition up the Tennessee. They went up as far as Florence, Ala., and all along the river route were greeted with cheers for the Union. The gun-boats captured three rebel steamers, and six others were burned by the secessionists.

Naval fight off Elizabeth City, N. C.: all the rebel gun-boats but one captured.

11. The great Sawyer gun at Newport News, Va.,

burst, killing two men and wounding four or five others.

Elizabeth City, N. C., occupied by the Union forces. It had been fired by the rebels and a great number of buildings destroyed.

12. Fort Donelson, on the Cumberland River, invested by 40,000 Union troops under Grant. There were about 18,000 rebels in the fort.

Skirmishes between the advance of Gen. Curtis' army and Price's men near Springfield, Mo., and in each the rebels were driven back.

Union forces took possession of Edenton, N. C.

A nest of guerrillas at Moorsfield, Va., broken up by the Union troops.

13. Attack on Fort Donelson commenced at 7.30 A.M. Battle lasted all day. At night the Union forces were reinforced by 8,000 men and four gunboats.

Union forces under Curtis took possession of Springfield, Mo., the rebels having evacuated it during the previous night, leaving in the hospitals 600 sick and wounded.

The House Treasury Note Bill with the legal tender clause passed the U. S. Senate.

Plymouth, N. C., occupied by Union troops.

Chesapeake and Albemarle Canal destroyed by the Union forces.

14. Battle of Fort Donelson renewed and continued all day.

Sec. of War ordered the release of all political prisoners on condition of their taking the oath of allegiance. The President proclaimed a general amnesty to all such as complied.

Return of Ames and Fish from Richmond. The

rebels refused to permit them to enter their lines, but agreed to exchange all the prisoners.

Cavalry reconnoissance to Blooming Gap, Va. Rebel camp broken up and several rebels killed and wounded.

15. Battle of Fort Donelson renewed and continued all day. At night the Union flag floated over the main redoubt, which completely commanded the inner fortifications.

Bowling Green, Ky., occupied by the Union troops under Gen. Mitchell.

Naval engagement near Fort Pulaski, Ga.

16. Fort Donelson surrendered to the Union forces. During the night Gens. Floyd and Pillow with 5,000 men had escaped, leaving Gens. Buckner and Tilghman with 13,000 men to continue the fight or surrender at discretion. The result was a surrender. Besides the prisoners, there were taken 3,000 horses, 48 field pieces, 17 heavy guns, 20,000 small-arms, and an immense amount of stores. Union loss during the three days' fighting: 446 killed, 1,735 wounded, and 150 prisoners. Rebel loss: 237 killed, 1,007 wounded, and 13,300 prisoners.

17. Battle of Sugar Creek, Ark.—rebels defeated.

18. First regular Congress of the Confederate States of America assembled at Richmond. It was composed of representatives from all the slaveholding States except Maryland and Delaware.

19. Rebel government ordered all the Union prisoners of war, numbering about 2,000, to be released.

Winton, N. C., attacked by the Union gun-boats and burned.

C. S. Congress at Richmond counted the electoral

votes for President and Vice-President which were given unanimously for Jefferson Davis, of Miss., and Alex. H. Stevens, of Ga. The number of votes by the States severally was as follows: Ala. 11, Ark. 6, Fla. 4, Ga. 12, La. 8, Miss. 9, N. Car. 12, S. Car. 8 Tenn. 15, Texas 8, and Virg. 18—total 106.

20. Clarkesville, Tenn., occupied by the Union forces. The rebels fled on the approach of the gun-boats, but succeeded in destroying the railroad bridge over Cumberland River.

Bentonville, Ark., occupied by Union troops.

A thousand rebels, sent to reinforce Fort Donelson, captured on their way down the river.

Gun-boat reconnoissance up the Occoquan River.

21. Nathaniel P. Gordon, convicted of trading in slaves, hung at New York. This was the first execution for the offense under the laws of the United States.

Skirmish near Independence, Mo.

Battle near Fort Craig, N. Mex.: fight lasted all day. Unionists loss 162 killed and 140 wounded. The rebels captured six pieces of artillery.

22. Jefferson Davis inaugurated President of the Confederate States for six years.

Martial law proclaimed over West Tennessee.

Day appointed by President Lincoln for a general movement of the land and naval forces.

23. Nashville, Tenn., evacuated by the rebels and occupied by the Union forces under Gen. Nelson.

Gallatin, Tenn., occupied by Union troops under Gen. Buell.

24. Fayetteville, Ark., captured by Union troops under Curtis. Part of the town burned by the rebels before evacuating.

Union army under Banks crossed the Potomac River at Harper's Ferry.

25. Telegraph lines taken possession of by the Government. Army news not to be published until authorized.

Skirmish at Mason's Neck, near Occoquan, Va.

Rebels (about this time) driven out of Texas, Dent, and Howell counties, Mo., by the Union cavalry.

26. Loan and Treasury Note (legal tender) Bill approved by the President.

27. Rebels begin to evacuate Columbus, Ky.

"Monitor" sailed from New York.

28. Rebel steamer "Nashville" ran the blockade at Beaufort, N. C.

Fast day in the Confederate States.

Charleston, Va., occupied by Union troops.

Rebels dispersed at Bird's Point, Mo.: 40 prisoners and six pieces of artillery captured by Union forces.

March, 1862.

1. John Minor Botts arrested at Richmond, Va., for treason to the Confederate States.

Schooner "British Queen" captured while endeavoring to run the blockade at Wilmington, N. C.

2. Union gun-boats engaged the rebel batteries at Pittsburg Landing, Tenn.: rebels repulsed with great slaughter.

Death of Gen. Fred. W. Lander.

Brunswick, Ga., captured by the Union forces.

3. Columbus, Ky. (the Gibraltar of the Confederacy), occupied by Union troops, the city having been previously evacuated by the rebels.

Mayor of Nashville issued a proclamation calling upon all citizens to return and resume their business under the protection of the federal authorities.

3. Brigham Young elected Governor of Deseret (Utah) under the constitution preparatory to asking admission into the Union.

4. Gen. Pope's troops engaged the rebels near New Madrid, Mo.

5. Bunker Hill, Va., occupied by Union troops.

Rebel schooner "Wm. Mallory" captured.

Beauregard assumed command of the rebel army in Mississippi.

6. President Lincoln asked Congress to declare by resolution that the United States ought to co-operate with any State which may adopt a gradual abolition of slavery, giving to such State pecuniary aid as indemnity.

Smithfield, Va., occupied by Union troops.

6–8. Battle of Pea Ridge: the rebels (35,000) under Ben McCulloch, and federals (22,000) under Curtis. Rebels completely routed after three days' hard fighting. Union loss—203 killed, 972 wounded, and 176 missing; rebel loss—1,100 killed, 2,400 wounded, and 1,600 prisoners. The Unionists took thirteen pieces of artillery. McCulloch was killed.

7. Centreville, Va., evacuated by the rebels.

Leesburg, Va., and the fort which guarded it taken possession of by the federals.

Fort Clinch and the towns of St. Mary's, Ga., and Fernandina, Fla., taken by a part of the Dupont Expedition.

8. The Army of the Potomac divided into five corps d'armée.

Beauregard called on the planters to send their bells to dépôts for conversion into cannon.

The rebel steamer "Merrimac" or "Virginia," accompanied by four or five gun-boats, coming from Norfolk, attacked the Union fleet lying in Hampton Roads. The U. S. frigate "Cumberland" was sunk; the "Congress" surrendered, and was burned; the "Minnesota" grounded, and the gun-boats "Oregon" and "Zouave" were badly damaged. The rebel ships returned to Elizabeth River.

9. The rebel steamers again appear in Hampton Roads. The U. S. battery "Monitor" having arrived on the evening of the 8th, entered into the contest, and fought the "Merrimac," the two vessels touching each other part of the time. The "Merrimac" at last gave up the contest, badly damaged and so much disabled as to require the aid of tugs to get her away. The "Monitor" was uninjured. As the first encounter of iron-clad vessels, this contest created much interest with maritime nations.

0. Centreville, Va., occupied by the Union forces. Scouts approached Manassas, and ascertained that the rebels had evacuated the place.

Gun-boat "Whitehall" destroyed by fire in Hampton Roads.

Rebel troops from Texas occupied Santa Fe, N. Mex.

11. Union troops entered the works at Manassas Junction.

Gen. McClellan relieved of the supreme command of the army, and appointed to that of the Army of the Potomac. Gen. Halleck received the command of the Department of the Mississippi and Gen. Fremont of the Mountain Department.

The resolution recommending gradual emancipation adopted by the House of Representatives.

Skirmish at Winchester: 1,200 rebels put to flight.

The city of St. Augustine, Fla., occupied by the federals.

12. Attack on the rebel forts near Paris, Tenn.: rebels routed.

Jacksonville, Fla., occupied by Union troops

Winchester, Va., occupied by Gen. Banks.

Forts in New York Harbor garrisoned.

Cavalry fight near Lebanon, Mo. Gen. Campbell (rebel) captured.

13. Joseph Holt and Robert Dale Owen appointed to audit claims against the United States.

Point Pleasant, Mo., captured by Pope's troops after a few days' skirmishing.

New Madrid was also evacuated by the enemy, who abandoned all their armament and supplies, valued at $1,000,000.

14. Battle of Newbern, N. C. After a heavy fight, the rebels evacuated, and the Union soldiers occupied the city. An immense amount of arms, ammunition, and stores were found in the fortifications.

General McClellan issued a patriotic address to his army.

15. Naval expedition left Cairo for Hickman, Ky.

Newton, Va., occupied by Banks' troops.

Fight at Salem, Ark.: rebels defeated.

16. Rebel camp at Pound Gap, in the Cumberland Mountains, attacked by Union forces under Gen. Garfield, and completely routed.

17. Night skirmish in Black Jack Forest, between Pittsburg Landing and Corinth, Miss.

18. Name of Fort Calhoun, at the Rip Raps, Hampton Roads, changed to that of Fort Wool.

Steamer "Nashville" escaped from Beaufort, N. C.

Rebel gun-boat sunk near New Madrid by a masked battery.

Gen. Dix assigned to the command of the Middle Department.

Acquia Creek, Va., occupied by the rebels.

20. An expedition of engineers from Gen. Pope's army, having reached Com. Foote's fleet above Island No. 10, started on its return, and commenced cutting the famous canal for the passage of gun-boats to New Madrid.

21. New cabinet of Jeff. Davis confirmed by the rebel Senate, viz.: Sec. of State, J. P. Benjamin, La.; Sec. of War, G. W. Randolph, Va.; Sec. of Navy, S. R. Mallory, Fla.; Sec. of Treasury, C. G. Memminger, S. C.; Attorney-General, Thomas H. Watts, and Postmaster-General, James H. Reagan, Tex.

Gen. Butler arrived at Ship Island.

Washington, N. C., occupied by Union troops.

Departments of the Gulf and the South created: Gen. Butler assigned to the first and Gen. T. W. Sherman to the latter.

22. Reconnoissance in force to Cumberland Gap, Tennessee.

Skirmish on the Strasburg Road, near Winchester, Va.: Gen. Shields slightly wounded.

23. Battle of Winchester, Va.: rebels defeated, with a loss of 869 killed, wounded, and missing; Union loss 115 killed and 450 wounded.

Fort Mason, N. C., invested by Union forces.

24. Rebel works on Skidaway and Green islands, in

Warsaw Sound, Ga., abandoned by the rebels and destroyed by the federal troops.

Engagement between two Union gun-boats and a rebel masked battery near Eastport, Tenn.

26. Fight at Hammonsville, Mo., between the rebels and State militia; also at Warrensburg, Mo., between Quantrell's guerrillas and the militia; rebels repulsed in both attacks.

Fight near Denver City, Col. Ter.: 50 rebel cavalry captured.

27. Skirmish near Strasburg, Va.

28. Battle of Valle's Ranch, 15 miles from Santa Fe, N. Mex.

Shipping Point, Va., occupied by federals.

Reconnoissance beyond Warrenton, Va.

29. Cavalry charge through Middleburg, Va., in pursuit of the rebels fleeing from that place.

30. Skirmish at Clinton, Mo.

31. Baltimore and Ohio Railroad reopened: it had been closed nearly a year.

Rebel camp at Union City, Tenn., dispersed, and a large amount of spoils captured.

April, 1862.

1. Gen. Banks drove the rebels from Woodstock, Va.

Battle at Putnam's Ferry, Ark.: rebel stores captured.

2. President Lincoln's emancipation and compensation resolution passed the Senate.

Severe storm on the Mississippi: great damage from Cairo to New Madrid, both to private and government property.

Thoroughfare Gap, Va., occupied by federalists.

A steamer passed through the new military canal from above Island No. 10 to New Madrid.

Action at Farmington, Miss.: battalion of 2d Illinois Cavalry surrounded by rebels, but they cut themselves through and escaped.

3. Col. Roberts, of the 42d Illinois Volunteers, with 50 picked men, surprised the upper battery, near Island No. 10, drove out the rebels, and spiked 10 guns.

Bill to abolish slavery in the District of Columbia passed the Senate by a vote of 29 to 14.

Appalachicola, Fla., surrendered to the Union forces.

4. Departments of the Shenandoah and Rappahannock created.

Rebels attack the Union forces at Pittsburg Landing, Tenn.

Pass Christian, on the Gulf coast, taken by the Union forces.

Army of the Potomac struck their tents and commenced their march toward the rebel fortifications at Yorktown, Va.

Action at Farmington, Miss.: rebels reinforced and federals retired.

5. Union army in front of Yorktown.

6. Battle of Pittsburg Landing or Shiloh commenced: federals fell back to the protection of the gun-boats.

Gun-boat "Pittsburg" ran the batteries at Island No. 10, under a terrific fire.

Gen. Mitchell's forces reached Shelbyville, Tenn.

7. Battle of Pittsburg Landing continued: federals being reinforced, retook the camps and batteries captured on the 6th, and secured a large number

of prisoners. The rebels retreated, and Gen. A. S. Johnson (rebel) was killed. Union loss—1,735 killed, 7,882 wounded, and 4,044 missing and prisoners. Over 3,000 rebels were buried on the field.

Island No. 10 surrendered, after sustaining a bombardment of 23 days. Nine batteries and 125 guns were given up, also 13 steamers and a floating battery, with wharf-boats, stores, etc.; 10,000 small-arms, 2,000 horses, 1,000 wagons, etc., and upward of 6,000 prisoners.

8. National Tax Bill passed the U. S. House of Representatives by a vote of 125 to 13.

9. Secretaries of War and Navy issued congratulatory orders on the late victories.

Fight near Elizabeth City, N. C.: 80 rebels captured.

Gen. Halleck left St. Louis to assume command of his department in the field.

10. Union forces on Tybee Island opened fire on Fort Pulaski, at the entrance of Savannah River.

11. Bill for the abolition of slavery in the District of Columbia passed the House of Representatives by a vote of 93 to 39.

Fort Pulaski, after sustaining a bombardment of 30 hours, surrendered unconditionally to Gen. Hunter. With the fort were taken 47 guns, 7,000 shot and shells, 40,000 pounds of powder, 360 prisoners with their small-arms and accoutrements, and a good supply of provisions.

Huntsville, Tenn., occupied, and 200 rebels captured; also, a number of locomotives, cars, etc.

The steamer "Merrimac," with several small war-vessels, appeared in Hampton Roads, but did no further damage than capturing three small vessels at Newport News.

12. Gen. Hunter declared all the slaves in Fort Pulaski and in Cockspur Island free.

Engagement at Monterey, Va.

13. Two bridges on the Mobile and Ohio Railroad destroyed by an expedition from Pittsburg Landing.

Com. Foote arrived with the Mississippi flotilla before Fort Wright or Pillow, 78 miles above Memphis

14. Gun and mortar boats opened fire on Fort Wright.

Batteries at Lowry's Point, on the Rappahannock, shelled out by Union gun-boats.

15. Gloucester, Va., shelled from the Union gun-boats.

Rebels cut the levee on the Arkansas side of the Mississippi, near Fort Wright, and caused immense destruction of property.

16. President Lincoln signed the bill for the abolition of slavery in the District of Columbia.

Union troops left Ship Island for New Orleans

Battle of Lee's Mills, near Yorktown.

Skirmish at Savannah, Tenn

17. Newmarket and Mount Jackson, Va., occupied by Gen. Banks' troops.

A part of McDowell's forces marched from Warrenton toward Fredericksburg, Va.

Skirmish on Edisto Island, S. C.

18. Running fight between McDowell's advance and the rebels, near Fredericksburg. Falmouth occupied by our forces.

Rebels at Yorktown repulsed in a night attack on the Union troops.

Bombardment of forts Jackson and St. Philip commenced by the gun-boats and sloops of war under

Com. Farragut, and the mortar fleet under Capt. Porter. The combined fleet numbered 51 vessels, carrying 286 guns.

19. Battle of Camden or South Mills, N. C.: the rebel intrenchments carried and the rebels routed.

Gen. Banks' advance occupied Sparta, Va.

Gen. Mitchell at I-u-k-a, Miss.

21. Santa Fé, N. Mex., evacuated by the Texans and occupied by the federals.

22. Gen. Banks' advance arrived at Harrisburg, Va.

C. S. Congress at Richmond incontinently broke up and dispersed.

23. Battle at Paratta, on the Rio Grande, N. Mex., resulting in the defeat of the enemy.

24. Forts Jackson and St. Philip passed by the Union fleet. They had been ineffectually bombarded for six days.

Destruction of the Dismal Swamp Canal completed.

25. Union fleet arrived before New Orleans.

Fort Macon, at Beaufort, N. C., surrendered after a bombardment of 11 hours.

26. Com. Farragut demands the surrender of New Orleans; the mayor replied that the city was at the mercy of the gun-boats.

Capture of a rebel outwork at Yorktown.

Fort Macon occupied.

27. The stars and stripes raised over the U. S. Mint at New Orleans.

Gen. Butler landed his troops above Fort St. Philip.

Severe skirmish near Newbern, N. C.

28. Forts Jackson and St. Philip surrendered to the Union forces.

Captured steamer "Ella Warley" arrived at Port Royal, S. C.

29. Bridgeport, Ala., captured by Union troops under Gen. Mitchell. Rebels burned the bridge and abandoned their arms and supplies.

Gen. Butler entered and took military possession of the city of New Orleans.

Rebel battery near Port Royal, S. C., captured.

Skirmish near Corinth, Miss.

30. Cannonading at Yorktown.

Rebels cut the telegraph wire at Huntsville, Ala., and attacked one of the brigades.

May, 1862.

1. Rebel battery at White Point, North Edisto Island, S. C., captured by Union troops.

Fight at Pulaski, Tenn.: 251 Union troops captured by rebel cavalry.

2. Gen. Butler took possession of the *True Delta* office in New Orleans.

3. Fight near Monterey, Tenn.: enemy put to flight, with severe loss.

Fight near Farmington, Miss.: enemy lost four pieces of artillery, several hundred muskets, camp equipage, etc. Two bridges were destroyed by the federals.

4. Yorktown, Va., evacuated by the rebels, and the works occupied by the Union forces. Rebels pursued and their rear guard overhauled near Williamsburg, when a brisk cavalry fight occurred, in which the rebels were repulsed, with considerable loss in killed and wounded. Union loss: 27 wounded. In the works at Yorktown were found

71 guns (spiked) and a large amount of ammunition, tents, etc.

Gloucester, Va., taken by federals.

British steamer "Circassian" captured near Havana, Cuba.

5. Battle of Williamsburg, Va.: fighting from early morning to 4 P.M., with varying successes and reverses; but finally the rebels were routed by the bayonet, and fled, leaving their dead and wounded on the field. Loss on both sides heavy. Union loss: 455 killed, 1,411 wounded, and 388 missing.

Skirmish at Lebanon, Tenn.: after a two-hours' fight the rebels retreated, leaving 105 prisoners, with their horses and arms.

6. Rebels evacuated Williamsburg, Va., during last night, leaving more than 1,000 wounded men in the hospitals. Town occupied by federals.

Rebels burned their gun-boats on York River.

Reconnoissance toward Harrisonburg, Va.: cavalry skirmish and retreat of the rebels toward the town.

7. Battle of West Point, Va.: the rebels attacked the Union troops landing from transports, but after a severe struggle were routed. The Union gun-boats took part in the action.

Flying rebels overhauled six miles beyond Williamsburg, and after a severe skirmish driven across the Chickahominy River.

President Lincoln visited Fortress Monroe and the fleet.

The "Merrimac" appeared off Craney Island and returned to Norfolk.

8. The iron-clad "Galena" and the gun-boats "Aroostook" and "Port Royal" started up the James

River; and the "Monitor," "Naugatuck," and several gun-boats left for Sewell's Point. The rebel "Merrimac" appeared, but refused to fight.

A troop of Union cavalry surprised and captured near Corinth, Miss.

Battle at McDowell, Va.: fighting from 6 A.M. to 9 P.M., when the federals retreated with a loss of 37 killed and 235 wounded.

9. Gen. Hunter (Department of the South) issued a manifesto declaring the slaves of South Carolina, Georgia, and Florida forever free.

Attack on Sewell's Point by the "Monitor," etc.

Battle of Farmington, Miss.: the rebels attacked the federal position, but though the Union forces were at first compelled to fall back, the fight resulted in a Union victory.

Rebels evacuated Pensacola, Fla.

Engagement at Slater's Mills, Va.

Bombardment of Fort Darling on the James River, Va.

10. Surrender of Norfolk, Va.: 5,000 Union troops landed at Willoughby Point and marched toward Norfolk. At 5 P.M. they were met by a delegation of citizens, who formally surrendered the city and also Portsmouth. The navy yard at Gosport was almost entirely destroyed by fire. The expedition was superintended by the President in person.

Craney Island abandoned by the rebels.

Naval fight near Fort Wright (or Pillow) between eight rebel and six federal gun-boats. The struggle was desperate. The enemy lost one of their boats by explosion, another by fire, and a third by sinking. The five remaining boats took refuge under the guns of the fort. Only one of the Union gun-boats was damaged.

Gen. Butler seized $800,000 in gold, in the office of the Netherlands consul at New Orleans. All the foreign consuls entered protests.

11. Rebels set fire to the "Merrimac" off Craney Island; she blew up at 5 A.M.

"Monitor" and other gun-boats proceeded to Norfolk.

Pensacola, Fla., occupied by Union troops. The navy yard and all the public buildings, except the custom-house, had been destroyed by the rebels before evacuating.

Rebel cavalry captured two locomotives and four cars at Cave City, Ky.

12. President Lincoln issued a proclamation declaring that the blockaded ports of Beaufort, N. C., Port Royal, S. C., and New Orleans, La., should be open on and after the 1st June for commercial intercourse.

Rebel steamer "Gov. Morton" captured.

Great destruction of tobacco on Elizabeth River.

13. McClellan's advance guard at White House, Va.

Armed rebel steamer "Planter," seven guns, run out of Charleston Harbor by a crew of eight negroes and surrendered to the blockading squadron.

Natchez, Miss., surrendered to the Union gun-boats.

15. Mounted guerrillas attack the Union railroad guard beyond Front Royal, Va.

16. Union gun-boats repulsed before Fort Darling, on James River.

Fast Day in the Confederate States.

Skirmishing near Corinth, Miss.

17. Naval expedition up the Pamunky River: rebels burned two gun-boats and a score of schooners.
   Skirmishing near Corinth, Miss.: enemy left 40 dead and 100 wounded. Union loss: 44 killed, etc.
   Rebels driven across the Chickahominy at Bottom's Bridge, which they burned, and secured their retreat.
18. Suffolk, 17 miles below Norfolk, occupied by federals.
   Skirmish at Yancey, Ark.
19. President Lincoln by proclamation repudiated the manifesto of Gen. Hunter liberating the slaves in his department.
   Reconnoissance to and skirmish at Clinton, N. C.
   The Mayor, Recorder, and Chief of Police of New Orleans arrested by Gen. Butler and sent to Fort Jackson.
20. Gen. McClellan's advance reached New Bridge, eight miles from Richmond: the whole army advancing.
21. Skirmishing along the whole Union lines near Corinth. Rebels uniformly driven back.
22. U. S. Senate organized itself into a High Court of Impeachment for the trying of W. H. Humphreys, a U. S. District Court Judge, on charges of treason presented by the House of Representatives.
23. Battle of Front Royal, Va., between Gen. Banks' advance and the rebels.
   Rebels defeated at Lewinsburg, Va.
   Rebels driven from Mechanicsville, near Richmond, Va.
24. Skirmishing near Corinth, Miss.
   Gen. Banks' forces retreated from Strasburg to Winchester, Va.

Battle at Bottom's Bridge, Chickahominy River: rebels repulsed.

Enemy routed at Ellison's Mills, and also at Cold Harbor, near Richmond.

25. Gen. Banks' forces retreated from Winchester to Martinsburg, Va., fighting all the way. Gen. Banks successfully covered his position and ammunition trains, all of which were saved. At sundown, the Union forces reached Williamsport.

26. Gov. Morgan, of New York, ordered a number of militia regiments to march immediately to Washington.

The Government, by proclamation, took military possession of all the railroads for the transportation of troops and munitions of war.

Additional troops called for by the Government.

Confiscation Bill passed the House of Representatives by a vote of 82 to 62.

Hanover C. H., Va., captured by federals.

Gen. Banks, with his whole force, crossed the Potomac River in safety.

Fighting before Corinth.

27. President Lincoln sent a message to Congress relating to Sec. Cameron's transactions.

Severe fighting before Corinth, in which the rebels suffered great loss.

28. Retreat of the rebels from Corinth commenced.

29. Corinth completely evacuated by the rebels, who retired in disorder.

Bridge 500 feet long over the South Anna River, Va., burned by the federals, who also captured Ashland, Va.

Skirmish at Pocotaligo, N. C.

30. Front Royal again occupied by Union troops: a large number of wagons, etc., captured.

Corinth, Miss., occupied by Union forces: the rebels had destroyed everything they could not carry away, and for five miles along their route the roads were filled with arms, etc. Over 2,000 prisoners were taken.

Rebels attacked Harper's Ferry, Va., but were driven off by the Union artillery.

31. Battle of Fair Oaks, Va.: rebels attacked the left wing of the Union advance, and after most desperate fighting the Union forces were driven back with great loss.

June, 1862.

1. Battle of Fair Oaks renewed: rebels driven at the point of the bayonet from the position they had gained the previous day, and two miles beyond. Loss (Union): 890 killed, 2,627 wounded, and 1,222 prisoners. Rebel loss in killed, wounded, and prisoners, 5,897.

2. Running fight between Fremont's command and Jackson's rebels on the road between Strasburg and Staunton, Va., Jackson being in full retreat. Rebels burned the Shenandoah Bridge at Mount Jackson.

Gen. Wool transferred from Fortress Monroe to the Department of Maryland, and Gen. Dix ordered to Fortress Monroe.

3. Fight six miles southwest of Corinth, and large haul of rebels.

Union troops landed on James Island, S. C.

4. Battle at Tranter's Creek, near Washington, N. C.
   Skirmish on James Island, S. C.
5. Union Mississippi flotilla (five gun-boats and eight rams) passed forts Wright and Randolph without resistance, and anchored about two miles above Memphis.
   Artillery battle at New Bridge, near Richmond: rebels retreated after two hours' fighting.
6. Great gun-boat fight before Memphis: fight commenced at daylight, and in less than two hours four of the enemy's gun-boats were disabled, and the other four in full retreat, followed by the Union boats, which captured three of them. The rebel flag-ship alone escaped. After the battle the city of Memphis unconditionally surrendered to the victors.
   Tax Bill passed the U. S. Senate by a vote of 37 to 10.
7. William B. Mumford executed at New Orleans for hauling down the U. S. flag from the Mint building, after it had been placed there by the Union soldiers.
   Battle at Union Church, near Harrisonburg, Virginia.
8. Battle of Cross Keys, near Port Republic, Va.: fighting lasted five hours, and ended in the retreat of the enemy. Union loss: 131 killed, 456 wounded, and 20 missing. Rebel loss: 500 killed and as many wounded.
9. Battle of Port Republic, Va., between Shields' and Jackson's forces: after a severe fight the federals were forced to retire, with the loss of two guns and a large number of killed and wounded.
10. Skirmish near James Island, S. C.

12. Fight near Village Creek, Jackson Co., Ark., in which the rebels were routed.
13. Union pickets driven in from Old Church, near Richmond.
Railroad behind McClellan's army, four miles from White House, cut by rebel cavalry. Great loss of material and two vessels burned.
14. Severe battle on James Island, S. C., about five miles from Charleston: Union troops repulsed with heavy loss.
16. Heavy skirmish before Richmond.
17. Battle between Union gun-boats and the rebel batteries at St. Charles, Ark., on White River. The Union forces carried the whole works. Steamer "Mound City" exploded her boiler, by which accident 125 men were killed or wounded.
Action at Fair Oaks: rebels driven off.
18. Rebel works at Cumberland Gap, Tenn., occupied by federals.
A law confiscating the slaves of rebels passed the U. S. House of Representatives by a vote of 82 to 54.
20. Com. Porter arrived off Vicksburg with 10 mortar-boats.
Free Territory Act signed by President Lincoln.
Holly Springs, Miss., occupied by Union troops.
24. Evacuation of White House, Va., commenced by McClellan. Gen. Hooker's division attacked by the rebels, who were repulsed at the point of the bayonet.
25. Battle of Oak Grove, a short distance from Fair Oaks, Virginia, on the Chickahominy: rebels repulsed.
Fight on the Memphis and Charleston Railroad;

rebels destroyed the train and captured several Union officers.

Gen. Butler ordered the seizure of the property of Gen. Twiggs in New Orleans.

26. The forces under Generals Fremont, Banks, and McDowell consolidated, and Gen. Pope assigned to chief command.

The Senate, as High Court, ordered and decreed that Judge Humphreys be removed from office and disqualified.

Battle near Mechanicsville, Va.: rebels 60,000 strong, under Jackson, advanced from Richmond, and succeeded in getting to the rear of McClellan's right wing. The battle raged furiously till night, and the Union troops were forced back a considerable distance. Loss on both sides severe.

Rebels destroyed their gun-boats on the Yazoo River.

27. Fremont relieved of his command at his own request.

Fight on Stewart's Plantation, in Jackson Co., Ark.: during the night the rebels retreated.

Battle near Mechanicsville renewed at 3 A.M.: fight lasted all day up to 9 P.M. The Union troops fell back to Gaines' Mill, where a desperate battle ensued. In the night the right wing of the Union army crossed the Chickahominy.

Bombardment of Vicksburg, Miss.

28. Evacuation of White House completed.

Eighteen loyal States, through their executive heads, petitioned the President to call out additional troops for the suppression of the rebellion.

Fighting on the Chickahominy continued: Union forces retreating in order.

29. Battles at Peach Orchard and Savage's Station.

The Union troops continue their retreat toward James River, their new base of operations, followed closely by the enemy.

30. Battle of White Oak Swamp: Union forces lost two batteries.

Battle of Charles City Cross Roads, about four miles from White Oak Swamp. The rebels were kept at bay by the gun-boats on James River. Loss heavy on both sides.

July, 1862.

1. Rebels (eight regiments) defeated by federals (two regiments) at Booneville, Mo.

Battle of Malvern Hill, the last of the seven days' fighting before Richmond. After a fierce battle, lasting two hours, the rebels were defeated. The total Union loss in all the fights was 15,224, viz., killed, 1,565, wounded 7,701, and missing 5,958.

Brunswick, Ga., established as a port of entry, and the port of Darien abolished.

Fight at Turkey Bend, on James River.

President Lincoln called for 600,000 volunteers to put down the rebellion.

2. President Lincoln signed the following bills: the Tax Bill, the Pacific Railroad Bill, and the Bill to Prohibit Polygamy in Utah.

Rebels made another attack on McClellan's position on James River, but were again repulsed, and retreated with considerable loss.

4. Eighty-sixth anniversary of American Independence celebrated throughout the loyal States in the grandest style.

Gen. McClellan issued an address to the Army of the Potomac congratulating them on their valor and endurance in having succeeded in changing their base of operations to James River, and promising them that they shall enter the capital of the South, etc.

5. Vigorous bombardment of Vicksburg.

6. Engagement at Duval's Bluffs: Union loss 22 killed and wounded; rebel loss 84 killed, wounded, and missing.

7. Battle of Bayou de Cache, Ark.: the advance of Gen. Curtis' army encountered 1,500 rebels, and after a desperate fight of two hours, put the enemy to flight, leaving 110 dead on the field. Union loss 7 killed and 57 wounded.

Engagement 10 miles above Duval's Bluffs: all the enemy's camp equipage and provisions captured.

8. President Lincoln arrived at Fortress Monroe and proceeded up James River.

Union expedition up Roanoke River started from Plymouth, N. C.

9. Rebel batteries at Hamilton, N. C. (Roanoke River), attacked and their forces routed: two or three steamers and schooners with supplies fell into the hands of the federals. Rebels left 30 or 40 dead on the field: Unionists lost two killed and eight or ten wounded.

10. Burnside's forces encamped at Newport News, Virginia.

11. Gen. Curtis' army, about which some apprehension had been felt, arrived safely at Helena, Ark.

President Lincoln appointed Gen. H. W. Halleck commander of all the land forces of the United States as general-in-chief.

Engagement of State militia and guerrillas at Pleasant Hill, Mo.: rebels defeated.

12. Gen. Albert Pike resigned his command in the Rebel army of the South-West.

13. Attack by 4,000 rebel cavalry on the Union troops at Murfreesboro, Tenn.: the Unionists made a gallant defense, but were overpowered by numbers and forced to surrender after losing 33 killed and 62 wounded. The rebel loss was greater. Gen. T. T. Crittenden was among the prisoners.

14. Gen. Pope assumed command of the Army of Virginia, and issued his famous orders discarding the idea of maintaining lines of retreat and base of support.

Battle of Fayetteville, Ark. Union forces 600 strong, under Major Miller, attacked the combined rebel forces of Rains, Coffee, Hunter, Tracy, and Hawthorne, about 1,600, nearly eight miles beyond Fayetteville, defeating and routing them completely. The enemy's camps were shelled, followed by cavalry charges, and their forces scattered, and the main body pursued for 12 miles.

15. Gen. Stevens' division from South Carolina arrived at Hampton Roads to reinforce McClellan.

Rebel iron-plated steam battery "Arkansas" came down the Yazoo and succeeded in running past the Union Mississippi flotilla and reaching the batteries of Vicksburg. During her passage a number of shots were exchanged, by which the "Arkansas" was considerably damaged and three of the federal vessels completely disabled, one having received a shot in her boiler. The "Arkansas" lost seven killed and 15 wounded. The number of shots received by the federal vessels were 73, by which 43 men were killed and 69 wounded.

17. In consequence of the great scarcity of small change in all parts of the country, Congress passed a law ordering the issue of postage and other stamps of the United States to be used as a currency. The law also made it a misdemeanor for individuals to issue shinplasters.

First regular session of the XXXVIIth Congress adjourned.

A portion of Gen. Pope's army entered Gordonsville, Va., unopposed, and destroyed the railroads.

Union troops at Cynthiana, Ky., attacked, and after a desperate fight of two hours overcome. The rebels occupied the town. Union loss 17 killed and 34 wounded; rebel loss 24 killed and 78 wounded.

18. Death of the rebel general D. E. Twiggs.

Engagement at Memphis, Mo., between 400 Union troops and 600 guerrillas: fight lasted three hours, and the Union troops were five times repulsed in as many different charges. In a sixth charge the rebels were completely routed, leaving 23 dead on the field. Union loss in killed and wounded 83.

A band of guerrillas made a raid upon Newburg, Ind., and robbed the hospital and committed other depredations.

19. Gen. Butler issued an order emancipating certain negroes.

20. Union expedition from Fredericksburg made a descent on the Virginia Central R.R., at Beaver Dam Creek, 35 miles from Richmond. The track and telegraph for several miles were destroyed

and the dépôt containing ammunition and stores was burned.

Union cavalry overtook Morgan's guerrilla band on the road from Mt. Sterling to Owensville, Ky., and after a two hours' fight scattered them, retaking the cannon and horses, etc., captured at Cynthiana. The rebels lost 25 in killed; Union loss 20 killed.

22. President Lincoln issued an order for the seizure of supplies necessary for army use in all the rebel States, and directing that persons of African descent should be employed as laborers, giving wages for their labor.

President Lincoln issued an order that foreigners should not be required to take the oath of allegiance.

Naval action before Vicksburg: by agreement between Commodores Davis and Farragut an attempt was made to capture the rebel ram "Arkansas." The fleet from below was to engage the lower batteries and the fleet from above the upper ones, while the gun-boats "Essex" and "Queen" were to attack the "Arkansas." During the engagement the "Arkansas" was several times run into and received numerous heavy shots. Both the federal gun-boats were shot through but received no material damage. "No one hurt."

23. Gen. Pope ordered the arrest of all disloyal male citizens within the lines of his command.

A cavalry expedition from Fredericksburg met and defeated a body of rebel cavalry stationed near Carmel Church, on the Telegraph Road, burned their camps, etc. An hour later a large body of Stuart's cavalry came up to attack them, and these, too, were defeated and driven across the North Anna River and pursued till within sight of Hanover Junction. The expedition passed over 70 miles in 29 hours, and returned with several prisoners, a large number of horses, and many arms, etc.

24. British steamer "Tubal Cain" captured.

25. Steamer "Cuba" ran the blockade into the port of Mobile.

President Lincoln issued a proclamation warning the rebels of the provisions of the Confiscation Act. The sixth section of the law allows the rebels sixty days within which to return to their allegiance, and failing to do so, their property becomes liable to seizure and forfeiture.

26. British steamer "Memphis" ran out of Charleston Harbor.

27. Steamer "Golden Gate," from San Francisco, 21st inst., with 230 passengers and treasure ($1,114,000 for New York and $270,000 for England), burned at sea near Manzanilla. All the treasure lost and 206 of the passengers. The news of this disaster had a considerable effect on the New York markets.

Reconnoissance in force in the direction of Kinston, N. C.

Gen. Pope left Washington to join his army.

28. Fight at Bollinger's Mills, Mo.: rebels lost 10 killed and many wounded, and several horses. guns, etc.

29. Rebels attack Mount Sterling, Ky., and are gallantly repulsed by the Home Guards. In their retreat they were met by a party of volunteers who drove them back toward the town, where

they were again well beaten by the Guards, who took all their horses and 48 prisoners.

Attack on Moore's Mills, near Fulton, Mo., by 900 guerrillas: after a fight of four hours the rebels were put to flight, leaving 62 dead and 100 wounded on the field. Union loss 16 killed and about 30 wounded.

30. A part of Commodore Porter's mortar fleet arrived in Hampton Roads.

Skirmish at Paris, Ky.: six companies of the 9th Pennsylvania Cavalry, after a march of two days and nights, overtook Morgan's guerrillas, drove in his pickets, and captured the town. Rebel loss 27 killed, 30 wounded, and 9 prisoners.

31. Attack on Sterling, Ky.: rebels lost 13 killed and 105 prisoners out of a band of 127.

Action at the bend of Languella River, Ark.: a regiment of Texas rangers surrounded a company of Union troops and killed, wounded, and captured all but 20, who escaped.

August, 1862.

1. Retaliatory order issued by the rebel government: Gen. Pope and his officers declared not to be entitled to the privileges of prisoners of war.

Rebel batteries on James River, opposite Harrison's Landing, opened fire on the Union transports and troops a little after midnight. Their fire was returned and before morning their batteries silenced. Union loss: 6 killed and 8 wounded.

Rebel attack on Newark, Mo.: Union troops (70) surrendered after fighting three hours with a loss of 4 killed and 4 wounded. Rebel loss over 100 killed and wounded.

2. Reconnoitering party from Pope's army crossed the Rapidan and took Orange C. H., Va., which was occupied by two regiments of rebel cavalry. Eleven of the enemy were killed and 52 taken prisoners. Union loss: 2 killed and 3 wounded.

Unionists came in force to Newark, Mo., and routed the guerrillas, who left everything they had captured the day previous.

Skirmish at Ozark, Mo.

3. Reconnoitering party from the Army of the Potomac advanced to within 14 miles of Petersburg, Va.

Rebel steamer "Columbia" captured with a valuable cargo.

4. President Lincoln ordered a draft for 300,000 militia to serve in the army of the United States for nine months; also a special draft from the militia in States whose quota of volunteers under the last call shall not be filled by the 15th August. A third article of this order relates to promotions for meritorious and distinguished services, the prevention of the appointment of incompetent and unworthy officers, and the expulsion from the service of such incompetent persons as now hold commissions.

5. Battle of Baton Rouge: a force of 6,000 rebels under Breckinridge attacked the Union forces under Williams stationed at Baton Rouge. A severe engagement ensued, and for a time the Unionists were driven from their position, but they soon rallied and forced the enemy to retreat 10 miles from the city, leaving their dead and

wounded, numbering between 300 and 400. Union loss: 81 killed, 257 wounded, and 31 missing. Gen. Williams was killed.

Naval engagement five miles above Baton Rouge: the gun-boat "Essex" (Porter) attacked the "Arkansas," and after a short engagement incendiary shot were thrown into her, and she was blown up and entirely destroyed.

Malvern Hill occupied by Union troops after a fight of two hours' duration. The federal gun-boats shelled a rebel encampment beyond Malvern Hill.

Gen. Robert McCook, while riding in an ambulance, being sick, assassinated by the rebels near Salem, Tenn.

Attack on Fort Donelson, Tenn.: the rebels 800 strong were repulsed with a heavy loss. The fort was garrisoned by 400 federalists.

6. Battle near Kirksville, Mo.: rebels routed with a loss of 150 killed and wounded, 40 prisoners, 200 stand of arms, 200 horses, and a number of wagons. Union loss: 5 killed and 32 wounded.

Gen. Hooker, commanding the federal troops, retired from Malvern Hill in the night.

7. British steamer "Ladona" captured.

Skirmish at Cumberland Gap, Tenn.: in the several engagements the rebels lost, in killed and wounded, 125 men; Union loss 3 killed, 15 wounded, and 50 prisoners. Large quantities of forage, tobacco, etc., captured, also horses and mules.

Fight near Fort Donelson, Tenn.: four companies of Union cavalry came up with the rebels about seven miles from the fort on the road to Clarkesville, strongly posted and in ambush. After half an hour's fighting the enemy retreated with great loss. Union loss 2 killed and 18 wounded.

Rebels crossed the Rapidan and advanced toward Culpepper C. H. and Madison C. H., Va.

8. Pope's advance fell slowly back, the federal forces concentrating at Culpepper C. H.

Battle near Fort Fillmore, N. Mex., between the rebels under Sibley and the federals under Canby. Sibley's forces were routed and all his men taken but 150 who escaped. Sibley himself was assassinated by his own men, who charged him with drunkenness and inefficiency.

U. S. Sec. of War issued an order to prevent the evasion of military duty, and suspending the writ of habeas corpus in respect to all persons arrested and detained under its provisions; also for the arrest and imprisonment of persons who by act, speech, or writing discourage volunteer enlistments, etc.

9. Battle of Cedar Mountain: Union troops (7,000) under Banks and rebels (12,000) under Jackson met at Cedar Mountain, near Culpepper C. H., Va. The battle raged from 4 P.M. until after dark, when both parties retired from the field. Union loss 73 killed, 357 wounded, and 41 missing.

10. Rebels retreat from Cedar Mountain before daylight, leaving their dead on the field. They fall back two miles from the Union front.

11. Several fights near Williamsport, Tenn., between guerrilla and Union forces, in each of which the rebels were defeated with considerable loss.

Engagement at Kinderhook, near Columbia, Tenn.: skirmishing continued four hours and resulted in the discomfiture of the rebels.

Independence, Mo., surrendered to the rebels. The Union officers refused to fight, but the soldiers entered into the engagement with determined bravery and were finally overpowered and surrendered.

12. Gallatin, Tenn., surrendered to Morgan's guerrillas, who captured four companies of federals, a train loaded with forage, and 60 horses. During the night the town was retaken.

Reconnoissance in force from Pope's army in the neighborhood of Slaughter Mountain.

13. Battle of Yellow Creek, Clinton Co., Mo.: rebels defeated, leaving 60 prisoners in the hands of the federals.

Collision between the steamers "Peabody" and "West Point" on the Potomac: about 80 lives (convalescent soldiers) lost.

14. Gen. Burnside's corps d'armée arrived at Fredericksburg.

15. Rebels made a feint to cross the Rapidan, but were driven back.

Fight at Lone Jack, Jackson Co., 20 miles west of Lexington, Mo.: the rebels succeeded in dispersing the Union forces.

16. Union army under McClellan evacuated Harrison's Landing, on the James River: advance reached Williamsburg.

Cols. Corcoran and Wilcox, Lt.-Col. Brown, and Major Rogers, after having been confined in military prisons for over a year, were released and arrived in the Union lines.

Battle of Lone Jack renewed: after a severe engagement the rebels were routed with great slaughter. Union loss: 43 killed, 154 wounded, and 75 missing. Rebels lost 118 killed and large numbers wounded.

17. McClellan's advance reached Hampton, Va.

18. Rear of McClellan's army crossed the Chickahominy.

Pope's retreat commenced.

C. S. Congress reassembled at Richmond.

19. Department of the Ohio formed of the States of Ohio, Michigan, Indiana, Illinois, Missouri, and Kentucky east of the Tennessee River, and including Cumberland Gap. Major-General H. G. Wright appointed to the command.

Cavalry expedition to Charleston, Mo.; rebel camp in White Oak Ridge, west of Hickman, attacked and routed, 4 rebels being killed and 19 taken prisoners, also 27 horses, 100 muskets, etc.

20. Clarkesville, Tenn., surrendered to the rebels without resistance, and large amounts of federal property seized. Col. Mason, the commander, was the same person denounced by Gen. Sherman for cowardice at Pittsburg Landing.

Sioux Indians attacked Fort Ridgely, Minn., and were repulsed.

Jackson's rebel forces crossed the Shenandoah at Berry's Ford and drove in the federal pickets at the river in the neighborhood of Brandy Station, between Culpepper and the Rappahannock.

21. Five rebel regiments crossed the Rappahannock on a pontoon bridge and almost walked into the masked batteries of Gen. Sigel, which opened upon them with canister and grape, mowing them down by scores: 700 of the enemy were killed and wounded, and upward of 2,000 made prisoners. Union loss very light.

Gallatin, Tenn., surrendered to the rebels: Union loss 26 killed, 35 wounded, and 200 prisoners; rebel loss 13 killed and 50 wounded. Federal prisoners released on parole.

22. Catlett's Station, Va., captured by Stuart's cavalry.

Skirmishing along the Rappahannock at various points all day with various successes and reverses: great slaughter on both sides.

23. At 4 A.M. the federal artillery opened upon the rebels from the left bank of the Rappahannock. Firing commenced near Bealton Station and soon extended along the whole line of the left wing. The rebels promptly replied. For several hours this terrific firing continued, and was probably the heaviest artillery duel ever fought on the continent. By 9 A.M. the firing somewhat abated, until it was finally stopped as if by mutual agreement.

24. Battle between Bloomfield and Cape Girardeau, Mo.: rebels routed, with the loss of 30 killed, 50 wounded, and 16 prisoners; also, arms, ammunition, equipage, etc.

25. Sharp skirmish at Waterloo Bridge, Va.

Stonewall Jackson left the rebel army with his force and took the direction of Manassas, which he approached through Thoroughfare Gap.

Rebels repulsed in an attack on Fort Donelson, Tenn.

26. Rebel cavalry reached Manassas, having marched 62 miles in less than two days. From Manassas they advanced nearly to within cannon-shot of Washington.

Combined naval and military expedition under Gen. Curtis and Com. Davis returned to Helena, Ark. The expedition captured the rebel transport steamer "Fair Play," containing 1,200 Enfield rifles, 4,000 muskets, a large quantity of ammunition, four field guns, etc. Col. Woods captured one rebel encampment with all their arms, etc., and another with tents, baggage, and provisions. The expedition proceeded up the Yazoo River, where it captured a battery of four guns, with 7,000 lbs. of powder and 1,000 rounds of shot and shell and grape.

27. Skirmish near Rienzi, Mo.

Gen. Hooker came upon the rebels at Kettle Run, near Manassas, and after a sharp action completely routed the enemy, capturing a large number of arms, etc.

28. Battle near Centreville, Va., between federals under McDowell and Sigel and rebels under Jackson. The enemy was completely routed, with the loss of 1,000 prisoners, many arms, and one piece of artillery.

Severe fight near Woodbury, Tenn.: rebels routed, with great loss.

Union forces evacuated Fredericksburg, Va.

29. City Point, Va., shelled and entirely destroyed by the Union gun-boats.

Battle at Groveton, near Bull Run, Va., between the Union army under Pope and a large force of rebels. It commenced at daylight and lasted until dark, at which time the enemy retreated. Col. Fletcher Webster was among the slain.

30. Battle of Bull Run renewed, and after another desperate fight Gen. Pope, after being outnumbered by heavy reinforcements of the enemy, was forced to fall back on Centreville with heavy loss.

Battle near Richmond, Ky., between 6,500 federals under Gen. Nelson and about 15,000 rebels under

Gen. K. Smith. After fighting desperately for four or five hours the federals were overpowered and forced to retreat, with a loss of 200 killed, 700 wounded, and 2,000 prisoners. The rebels also took nine pieces of artillery and a number of wagons. The federals fell back on Lexington.

Buckhannon, Va., entered and occupied by the rebels.

Battle at Bolivar, Tenn.: rebels routed.

31. Fight at Weldon, Va.: rebels badly whipped, leaving 110 dead on the field. Union loss: 5 killed and 40 wounded.

September, 1862.

1. Legislature of Kentucky, from fear of rebel raids, adjourned from Frankfort to Louisville.

Bull Run Bridge, on the Orange and Alexandria Railroad, burned for the third time during the war.

Paris and Lexington, Ky., evacuated by the Union forces. Great excitement in Louisville in anticipation of an attack.

Battle near Chantilly, two miles from Fairfax C. H., Va., between Pope and Jackson. Union loss heavy. Gens. Kearney and Isaac J. Stevens were killed in the engagement.

Battle at Britton's Lane, near Estanaula, Tenn. The rebels, estimated at 5,000 strong, were opposed to a Union force of 800. After a fight of four hours the rebels fled.

Fight near Jackson, Tenn.: rebels left 110 dead, and their wounded were estimated at 250.

2\. Major-Gen. McClellan placed in command of the fortifications at Washington and all the troops for the defense of the national capital.

Martial law declared in Cincinnati, and all citizens ordered under arms, in consequence of the reported approach of a large force of rebels.

Considerable fighting between Fairfax C. H. ana Washington. The rear guard consisted of Hooker and Porter's commands, and did effectual service in keeping the rebels in check as the Union troops were moving into the fortifications protecting Washington on the Virginia side.

Plymouth, N. C., attacked by 1,000 rebels. After fighting about half an hour the rebels fled, having lost 30 killed and 40 prisoners. The Unionists lost three killed.

3\. Gen. White (Union) entered Harper's Ferry with his forces from Winchester, Va.

Centreville, Va., evacuated by the Union forces, which fell back on Washington.

4\. Rebel steamer "Oreto" ran the blockade into Mobile Bay, escaping the Union steamer "Oneida" in pursuit.

5\. A large part of the rebel army crossed over into Maryland during the night. They forded the Potomac near the mouth of the Monocacy and at two or three other points.

6\. Rebels in Maryland: a large force under Gen. Lee entered and occupied Frederick City.

Rebel cavalry attacked the Union outposts at Martinsburg, Va., and after a short engagement were defeated.

Union garrison at Washington, N. C., attacked by 1,200 rebels: after a fight of two hours the enemy were repulsed and pursued seven miles, with the loss of four guns and numerous prisoners. During the action the Union gun-boat "Picket," which was rendering assistance, exploded her magazine, killing 19 men and wounding six others.

7. Gen. McClellan left Washington under orders to drive the rebels from Maryland, most of his force having preceded him. He established his headquarters at Rockville, Md.

Bowling Green, Ky., occupied by the federal advance guard.

8. Gen. Pope relieved of the command of the Army of Washington and assigned to that of the North-West.

Gen. Lee issued his celebrated proclamation to the people of Maryland.

Fight at Poolesville, Md.: rebels scattered.

Indian fight at the lower agency in Minnesota, in which the red-skins were repulsed with considerable loss. The whites lost 14 killed and 45 wounded.

Fight near Cochran's Cross Roads, Miss., between 370 Unionists under Col. Grierson and 800 rebels under Jackson and Pierson. Rebels driven two or three miles through heavy timber.

8. Restrictions on travel rescinded and arrests for disloyalty, etc., forbidden, except by direction of the judge-advocate at Washington.

9. Col. Grierson attacked the rebels at Coldwater, Miss., and forced them to retreat.

Rebel cavalry attacked the Union force stationed at Williamsburg, Va., but were repulsed.

Evacuation of Fredericksburg, Va., by the rebels commenced.

10. Gov. Curtin, of Pennsylvania, issued an order calling on all able-bodied men in the State to organize immediately for defense.

Cavalry reconnoissance to Sugar Loaf Mountain, Md.

Large force of rebels at New Market, eight miles from Frederick City, Md.

Attack by the rebels on the Union troops near Gauley, Va.

Skirmish near Covington, Ky.

Great excitement in Cincinnati: 3,000 laborers ordered to the trenches—the rebels 16,000 strong believed to be approaching the city.

11. The Unionists, hard pressed by the rebels at Gauley, burned all the Government property and evacuated the place.

Maysville, Ky., taken by the rebels.

Bloomfield, Mo., attacked by the rebels and abandoned by the militia.

Hagerstown, Md., occupied by rebel troops.

Union cavalry (Pleasanton's) crossed the Monocacy near the Potomac.

Sugar Loaf Mountain, Md., occupied by the federal forces.

Rebel cavalry raid into Westminster, Md.

Federal forces stationed at Solomon's Gap, near Harper's Ferry, were driven in by the enemy.

Gen. McClellan called for reinforcements.

12. After the retreat from Gauley, the federals made a stand on Elk River, and had another desperate fight with the rebels, which lasted nearly all day. The salt works in Kanawha County destroyed, and Charleston shelled and burned.

Union forces entered and reoccupied Frederick City, and found there 450 sick rebels.

The rebels that took Bloomfield, Mo., attacked, and the town recaptured.

Harper's Ferry invested by the rebels.

Reconnoissances in force from Cincinnati found that the enemy had fallen back.

13. Eureka, Mo., captured by the federals.

Rebels opened attack on Harper's Ferry: artillery fighting all day.

Union forces drove the rebels from Middleton, Md.

Rebel army threatening Cincinnati fell back beyond Florence.

14. Battle of South Mountain, Md.—Gen. McClellan attacked the main body of the rebel army, when a general engagement ensued. Rebels fell back slowly, contending stubbornly for every inch of ground. In this way the battle raged furiously all day. In the night the rebels retreated toward the Potomac. Union loss: 443 killed, 1,806 wounded, and 76 missing—total 2,325. Gen. Reno was among the killed.

At 2 A.M. Maryland Heights were abandoned. The rebels attacked the federal left on Bolivar Heights but were repulsed. In the night the federal cavalry escaped from Harper's Ferry.

Rebels attacked Munfordsville, Ky., with artillery, and subsequently attacked the Union troops, but were repulsed five successive times.

15. The President assigned the following-named generals to the command of the army corps—1st corps, Hooker; 2d, Sumner; 3d, Heintzelman; 4th, Keys; 5th, Fitz John Porter; 6th, Franklin; 7th, Dix; 8th, Wool; 9th, Burnside; 10th, Mitchell; 11th, Sedgwick; and 12th, Sigel.

Harper's Ferry surrendered: 11,500 federals were

taken prisoners and parolled, and 60 pieces of cannon fell to the enemy. The cavalry from Harper's Ferry reached Greencastle, Pa., having captured an ammunition train belonging to the rebels.

Rebel invading army fell back toward Sharpsburg, Md.: during the retreat considerable skirmishing took place without any general result. The enemy were, however, driven from all their positions.

Business resumed at Cincinnati.

16. Battle at Munfordsville, Ky., renewed: desperate fighting throughout the day.

Rebel invading army made a stand on Antietam Creek, four miles from Sharpsburg. Terrific fighting, but the day closed without result.

17. Battle of Antietam. The battles of yesterday and to-day were the most furious and obstinate of the war, and the carnage on both sides terrible. The rebels were defeated and the federal army left in possession of the field. Each army numbered about 100,000 men—the federals under McClellan, Hooker, Porter, and Burnside; and the rebels under Lee, Jackson, Longstreet, and Hill. Union loss was 12,469, viz., 2,010 killed, 9,416 wounded, and 1,043 missing; rebel loss, 25,542.

Union reconnoissance toward Leesburg, Va.; rebels driven back at the point of the bayonet.

Cumberland Gap, Ky., evacuated by the Union forces under Gen. G. W. Morgan: though surrounded by the enemy, he succeeded in saving his command, which reached Greenupsburg on the 3d October. Before leaving, everything was destroyed.

Munfordsville, Ky., surrendered to the rebels: 4,600 Union troops made prisoners.

Frightful explosion at Pittsburg (Pa.) Arsenal: between 70 and 30 persons killed.

Union cavalry captured 450 rebel soldiers at Glasgow, Ky.

18. Another fast and prayer day observed in the Confederate States.

Rebels under a flag of truce bury the dead on the field of Antietam.

Prentiss, Miss., shelled and burned.

The proximity of the rebels to the Pennsylvania border caused the Governor to call the militia to arms: over 75,000 men responded.

19. Rebels evacuated Harper's Ferry: before leaving they burned all the Government property.

By daylight the main body of the rebels with their artillery had crossed the Potomac into Virginia and our cavalry entered Sharpsburg. In their retreat 3,000 rebels were made prisoners. Union victory complete!

Owensboro, Ky., attacked by guerrillas, who were driven off by the Union troops. Rebels lost 28 killed and 25 wounded, and the federals 3 killed and 18 wounded.

20. Battle of I-u-k-a, Miss. Rebel loss 1,438, viz., 385 killed, 692 wounded, and 361 prisoners; Union loss 749, viz., 144 killed, 565 wounded, and 40 missing. Besides considerable quantities of stores, the federals captured 1,629 stand of small-arms and 13,000 rounds of ammunition.

Rebels routed near Munfordsville, Ky., leaving 51 dead on the field.

Commander G. H. Preble, U. S. N., dismissed the service for allowing the steamer "Oreto" to escape him at Mobile.

21. A Union brigade crossed the Potomac into Virginia at Shepherdstown and encountered a large rebel force. The federals maintained their position for about two hours and captured four pieces of artillery, but were finally forced to recross the river with a loss of 150 killed, wounded, and missing.

Munfordsville, Ky., reoccupied by the federals.

Arrival of the advance Union fleet at Galveston, Tex.

Reconnoissance beyond Chantilly, Va.

Cavalry fight near Lebanon Junction, Ky.

22. President Lincoln's Emancipation Proclamation issued, declaring the slaves in any State in rebellion on the 1st of January, 1863, thenceforward and forever free.

Pennsylvania militia recalled and disbanded.

Battle of Wood Lake, Minn., with the Indians.

23. The sixth section of the Confiscation Act went into practical operation.

Col. Sibley's command attacked by the Sioux Indians in Minnesota. The Indians were repulsed with the loss of 30 killed and a large number wounded.

24. Convention of the Governors of the loyal States at Altoona, Pa.: they sat with closed doors and adopted an address to the President indorsing all the acts of the Government.

President Lincoln issued a proclamation suspending the writ of habeas corpus in respect to all persons arrested and imprisoned in any fort, camp, arsenal, military prison, or other place by any military authority, or by sentence of court-martial, etc.

Great excitement in Louisville, Ky.: business suspended and all required to labor on the fortifications.

Engagement at Donaldsonville, La.

25. Union reconnoissance to Warrenton Junction.

Commodore Wilkes' fleet arrived at St. George, Bermuda, and was notified to leave in 24 hours. Notice disregarded, he not leaving port until 3d October.

27. Augusta, Ky., 40 miles from Cincinnati, attacked by 600 mounted rebels and the town destroyed. The Union garrison of 120 men fired from the buildings and killed and wounded 90 rebels. The garrison finally surrendered, having lost 9 killed and 15 wounded.

28. British steamer "Sunbeam" captured by the Union gun-boats while attempting to run the blockade at Wilmington, N. C.

29. Major-Gen. Nelson shot and killed at the Galt House, Louisville, Ky., by Brig.-Gen. Jefferson C. Davis. The affair grew out of some personal difficulty.

Gen. Buell ordered to turn over the command of his army to Major-Gen. Thomas.

Warrenton, Va., taken by the federals.

30. Retaliatory resolutions introduced in the C. S. Congress on account of the Emancipation Proclamation of President Lincoln.

October, 1862.

1. Gen. Halleck sent to Gen. McClellan urging him to cross the Potomac at once, and give battle to the enemy.

Union expedition crossed the Potomac at Sheperdstown and drove the rebels to Martinsburg.

Western gun-boat fleet transferred from the War to the Navy Department.

Naval and military expedition under Gen. Brannan sailed from Hilton Head, S. C., bound south.

The federals left Louisville in search of the approaching enemy.

2. Union expedition from Hilton Head arrived in St. John's River, Florida, and the gun-boats opened fire on the rebel fortifications on St. John's Bluff.

3. Troops landed from the Florida fleet surprised two rebel camps and captured a large number of arms and a quantity of supplies and ammunition. The enemy's works on St. John's Bluff reduced.

President Lincoln reviewed the Army of the Potomac.

The combined rebel forces made a demonstration toward Corinth, Miss., and drove in the Union pickets.

Union Gen. G. W. Morgan reached Greenupsburg, Ky., 15 miles from Portsmouth, Ohio, with his force from Cumberland Gap, having marched 219 miles in 16 days.

Rebel Gen. Morgan repulsed near Olive Hill, Ky.

4. Rebels early A.M. renewed their attack on the Union forces at Corinth, Miss. The fighting was desperate, and at one time the rebels had penetrated to the public square of the town. Finally they were driven at the point of the bayonet. Union loss 2,359, viz., 315 killed, 1,812 wounded, and 232 prisoners. Rebel loss 9,363, viz., 1,423 killed, 5,692 wounded, and 2,248 prisoners.

Union troops from Louisville reached Bardstown,

driving the enemy's rear guard and continuing the pursuit toward Springfield.

5. Rebels retreating from Corinth, Miss., reached the Hatchee River, where they were attacked by the federals and lost two batteries and 400 prisoners. Loss on both sides heavy.

Galveston, Texas, occupied by the federal forces.

6. Gen. Halleck peremptorily ordered Gen. McClellan "to cross the Potomac and give battle to the enemy or drive him south. Your army must move now while the roads are good."

Battle of Lavergne, Tenn., between a detachment of Union troops from Nashville and the rebels under Anderson and Gov. Harris. The fight lasted only 30 minutes, when the rebels fled with the loss of 80 killed and wounded, and 175 prisoners. Union loss 5 killed and 9 wounded.

British mail steamer "Merlin" brought to off the harbor of St. George by a shot from one of Com. Wilkes' vessels.

7. Expedition to destroy the salt-works of the rebels on the coast of Florida.

Union army arrived within two miles of Perryville, Ky., where the enemy was found in force.

Union reconnoissance to the Rappahannock through Centreville and Manassas Junction.

Rebels evacuated Lexington, Ky.

8. Battle of Perryville, Ky. A desperate fight took place at Chaplin's Hills, near Perryville, between the federals under Rousseau and the rebels under Bragg, Buckner, Cheatham, and Marshall. The fight lasted all day with varying success, both sides suffering severely in killed and wounded.

9. Battle of Perryville renewed. Before the close of

the day the enemy were driven 10 miles with great slaughter and became entirely routed. Union loss: 468 killed, 1,463 wounded, and 161 missing. Rebel loss known to have far exceeded that of the federals: 640 dead rebels were buried by the Union troops. The federals captured 17 guns, 500 prisoners, and 106,000 rounds of ammunition.

Stuart's rebel cavalry started on their famous expedition to Pennsylvania. The force consisted of 1,800 mounted men and four pieces of horse artillery. The troops rendezvoused at Darksville at 12 M., and marched thence to Hedgeville, where they encamped for the night.

10\. Stuart's rebel cavalry reached Chambersburg, Pa., at 6 P.M., having crossed the Potomac at McCoy's, between Hancock and Williamsport.

Federals returned from the pursuit of Price's rebels, reporting them dispersed, demoralized, and incapable of further mischief.

11\. Stuart's cavalry burned the machine shops and destroyed the rolling stock of the Cumberland Valley R.R. at Chambersburg, and after seizing about 500 horses and a quantity of Government clothing left the town, and escaped across the Potomac in the vicinity of Edward's Ferry into Virginia.

Gen. Wool arrived at Harrisburg and assumed command of the troops for the defense of the State.

Rebels in large force appear before Nashville, Tenn., and demand the surrender of the city, which was refused.

The whole rebel army engaged in the battle of Perryville reached Bryantsville, Ky., the Union forces slowly following.

Skirmish near Lagrange, Ark.: rebels defeated.

Battle between Harrisburg and Danville, Ky., in which the rebels were defeated and made tracks for Camp Dick Robinson.

12. Stuart's cavalry occupied Leesburg, Va. They appeared exceedingly well clothed in U. S. uniforms captured during their raid into Pennsylvania.

13. C. S. Congress adjourned to meet again on the 2d Monday in January, 1863.

Bragg's army evacuated Camp Dick Robinson, Ky.

14. State elections held in Pennsylvania, Ohio, and Indiana: Republicans defeated by decided majorities, and Conservatives elected in their places.

A donation of $100,000 received from San Francisco, Cal., by the Sanitary Commission.

Federalists pursuing Bragg's army, and considerable fighting during the day.

15. Heavy fight between Lexington and Richmond, Ky., in which 45,000 rebels were repulsed by 18,000 federals. The federals reached Crab Orchard. Rebel loss: 1,300 killed and 2,000 wounded. Union loss: 600 killed and 2,300 wounded.

16. Pursuit of Bragg in Kentucky virtually abandoned.

Charleston, Va., occupied by Union forces.

British steamer "Wachuta" captured after an all-day's chase off the coast of North Carolina.

Union reconnoissance up the Appalachicola River, Fla.: expedition captured a sloop laden with cotton.

17. Return of the expedition sent out yesterday to Bolivar Heights. They found the enemy in force at Princetown, five miles from Winchester Va., and captured 1,500 bushels of corn.

Two companies of Union infantry and a company of

cavalry from Island No. 10, in the Mississippi River, encountered 300 rebel cavalry on the Arkansas side, and had a brilliant skirmish. During the engagement two parties of rebels by mistake fired into each other and thus aided the federals in subduing both.

18. Rebels 1,500 strong under Morgan dashed into Lexington, Ky., and took 125 prisoners.

A powerful iron steamer during the night ran the blockade of Charleston.

19. Morgan pursued through Lawrenceville, Ky.

Fighting near Nashville.

20. At 3 A.M. 300 or 400 rebels destroyed a Union train of 81 wagons near Bardstown, Ky. At daylight they captured another train in Bardstown.

21. An expedition from McClellan's army intercepted a force of rebel cavalry foraging near Lovettsville, Loudon Co., Va., and killed 15 and captured 32 of them.

Gen. Jeff. C. Davis, who was arrested for killing Gen. Nelson, released and ordered to report for duty at Cincinnati.

Expedition consisting of 4,000 or 5,000 men with artillery and 15 transports and gun-boats left Hilton Head for a reconnoissance along the Charleston and Savannah Railroad.

Rebels near Nashville attacked and dispersed.

22. Governor of Kentucky called on the people of Louisville to defend the threatened city.

Federals attacked Pocotaligo and Coosawatchie, S. C., and succeeded in reaching the Charleston and Savannah Railroad. The expedition was engaged in a desperate fight with the rebels, who were driven four miles.

Battle of Maysville, Ark. (second battle of Pea Ridge): federals attacked 5,000 or 6,000 rebels, and after an hour's hard fighting totally routed them, with the loss on the part of the rebels of all their artillery, a battery of six-pounders, and a large number of horses. By this battle all the organized forces of the rebels were driven back to the Valley of the Arkansas.

23. About 200 federals attacked by 800 rebels near Waverly, Tenn., 20 miles west of Fort Donelson. The latter were completely routed.

24. Gen. Buell removed from the command of the army in Kentucky, and Gen. Rosecrans assigned to the command.

Rebels repulsed at Brownsville, Tenn.

Skirmish at Morgantown, Kentucky: 16 rebels captured.

British steamer "Scotia," loaded with arms, powder, etc., captured at Bull's Bay, S. C.

Gen. Weitzel's brigade, 6,000 strong, left Carrollton, above New Orleans. The expedition was made up of transports and gun-boats.

25. Cavalry skirmish at Manassas Junction and Bristol Station.

Rebels routed at Greenville, Mo.

Gen. Sherman issued a stringent order for the government of the city of Memphis, Tenn.

26. Advance of the Army of the Potomac commenced at Harper's Ferry.

Gen. Burnside's division crossed into Virginia.

Gen. Weitzel's expedition landed at Donaldsonville: a sharp engagement with the rebels followed, during which the federals took one piece of artillery and 218 prisoners.

27. Rebels (1,500) attacked and defeated at Putnam's Ferry, Mo.

British steamer "Anglia" captured four miles inside of Bull's Bay, S. C.

Rebel army under Echols, Floyd, and Jenkins retreated from Charleston, Va.

Battle of Labadieville, on Bayou Lafourche, La. The rebels were put to flight after a short resistance. Rebel loss 6 killed, 15 wounded, and 208 prisoners; Union loss 18 killed and 74 wounded.

28. Halltown, Va., occupied by Union troops.

Camp of 3,000 rebels near Fayetteville, Ark., attacked by 1,000 federals, and after a sharp fight completely routed, leaving all their equipage. Rebels pursued into the Boston Mountains.

Skirmish at Snicker's Gap, Va.

29. Skirmishing at Upperville and Paris, Va. Federals pass Snicker's Gap.

Great fire at Harper's Ferry: 26 cars loaded with hay burned and part of the railroad bridge destroyed.

30. Gen. Rosecrans arrived at Louisville.

Gen. O. M. Mitchell, in command of the Department of the South, died of yellow fever at Beaufort, S. C.

31. Skirmish at Marysville, Va.

Advance guard of the column for the relief of Nashville passed through Bowling Green, Ky.

November, 1862.

1. Artillery fight at Philomont, Va., lasting five hours. Rebels pursued toward Bloomfield, when another skirmish ensued, lasting nearly four hours (Sunday), when the rebels finally decamped.

Rebel steamer "A. B. Ligur" captured near New Orleans.

2. Gen. Foster's expedition from Newbern, N. C., took up its line of march.

Federals being reinforced, took possession of Snicker's Gap, Va.

3. Federals drove the enemy out of Thoroughfare Gap and took possession of it.

Upperville, Va., occupied after a splendid engagement lasting four hours.

Reconnoissance through Snicker's Gap to view the country west of the Blue Ridge. At the base of the mountain, close by the banks of the Shenandoah, was found a large force of rebels, who were literally driven into the river and drowned by scores.

4. Ashby's Gap, Va., occupied by federals.

Elections in several States resulted in the choice of Conservatives.

Major Reid Sanders, C. S. A., captured on the coast of Virginia, while endeavoring to escape with rebel dispatches.

Gen. McClellan's headquarters at Upperville.

La Grange, Miss., entered by Union troops.

Engagement at Markham, Va.

Salt-works at Kingsbury, Ga., destroyed by federals.

5. Nashville, Tenn., attacked by the rebels, who were signally repulsed.

Skirmish between the cavalry forces of Pleasanton and Stuart at Barbour, Va.: rebels driven.

Galveston, Tex., surrendered and occupied by federals.

Gen. McClellan relieved from the command of the Army of the Potomac, and Burnside appointed his successor.

6. Warrenton, Va., occupied by the advance of the federal army.

Federal reinforcements arrived at Nashville, Tenn.

Fighting at Garrettsburg, Ky.

7. Union expedition up Sapello Sound, partly made up of negroes.

8. Skirmish at Little Washington, Va.

Cavalry charge on the rebels near Gaines' Cross Roads.

Fight at Old Lamar, near Holly Springs, Miss.

9. Union gun-boats shelled and destroyed the town of St. Mary's, Ga.

Gen. Butler sequestrated the property in the parish of Lafourche, La., and declared all sales made by disloyal persons since the 18th September void.

10. Gen. Rosecrans arrived at Nashville.

Capt. Dahlgren, with 54 men from Gen. Sigel's body guard, made a brilliant dash into Fredericksburg, Va., which was garrisoned by nearly 500 rebels. So sudden was the surprise that the enemy could not be collected, and after an attempted defense of short duration by detached parties, the rebels fled, leaving their killed and wounded and 34 prisoners. The attacking party lost but one man killed and one wounded.

Gen. Halleck ordered all absentee officers to their regiments.

Great Union demonstration in Memphis.

Mt. Gilead, Va., attacked by rebel cavalry and 35 federals captured.

11. Gen. Rosecrans' command arrived at Fort Donelson.

12. Gen. Grant's advance reached Holly Springs, Miss., after a slight skirmish.

Rebels routed at Madisonville, Ky., with a loss of 25 killed and 60 prisoners, etc.

13. Skirmish near White Sulphur Springs, Va.

15. Army of the Potomac, under Gen. Burnside, took up its line of march from Warrenton toward Fredericksburg, Va.

Gen. A. J. Hamilton appointed military governor of Texas.

Artillery fight near Fayetteville, Va.

16. Gen. Burnside moved his headquarters to Catlett's Station, Va.

17. Artillery engagement near Fredericksburg, Va.

President Davis ordered retaliation for the execution of ten rebels in Missouri.

The C. S. steamer "Alabama" arrived at Martinique. The U. S. frigate "San Jacinto" arrived at the same place, but immediately went outside the harbor to await her reappearance.

18. Army of the Potomac reached Falmouth, opposite Fredericksburg, Va.

Skirmish at Rural Hill, Va.

The C. S. steamer "Alabama" escaped from Martinique.

19. Federal pickets driven in at Suffolk, Va.

Stuart's rebel cavalry at Warrenton Junction.

First General Council of the Protestant Episcopal Church of the Confederate States of America met at Augusta, Ga.

20. Skirmish at Charlestown, Va.

21. Gen. Sumner demands the surrender of Fredericksburg, Va. In case of refusal, 16 hours should be given for the removal of women and children.

22. The War Department issued an order releasing persons who had been imprisoned for resisting the

draft, discouraging enlistments, etc.; and also parolling persons who had been sent from the rebel States by the military commanders or governors.

Gen. Francis E. Patterson committed suicide.

24. Scouting parties left camp near Charlestown, Va., and marched 210 miles in 70 hours.

25. Rebel raid into Poolesville, Md.

A body of 4,000 rebels attacked Newbern, N. C., but were forced to retreat in disorder.

26. President Lincoln visited Gen. Burnside at Belleplaine, Va.

Successful reconnoissance from Bolivar Heights, Va.

Rebel camp at Cold Knob, Va., surprised.

27. Nearly all the political prisoners released from the forts and government prisons.

Railroad from Acquia Creek to Falmouth, Va., completed.

Rebels defeated near Frankfort Va., and 110 taken prisoners.

Thanksgiving observed in the loyal States with unusual solemnity.

28. Battle of Cane Hill, Ark.: Gen. Blunt with 5,000 Union troops attacked the rebel forces under Gen. Marmaduke, and after an engagement of three hours the enemy broke and ran. The Union troops pursued, and a running fight was kept up for a distance of 12 miles. The rebels lost 60 men: federal loss small.

Gen. Grant's army struck their tents and marched in the direction of Holly Springs.

A large body of rebel cavalry crossed the Potomac and made a descent upon two companies of the 3d Pennsylvania cavalry, near Hartwood, capturing nearly the whole force.

29. Gen. Stahl's force reached Berryville, Va., *via* Snicker's Gap, where they had a skirmish with the rebels, who were completely routed, and lost all their camp equipage, 50 killed and wounded, 40 prisoners, etc. Union loss, 15 killed and wounded.

30. U. S. steamer "Vanderbilt" returned from an unsuccessful cruise after the rebel steamer "Alabama."

An expedition under Gen. Hovey left Helena, Ark., for the South.

December, 1862.

1. The third session of the XXXVIIth Congress commenced at Washington.

Tallahatchie, Miss., evacuated by the rebels.

2. King George C. H., Va., surprised and captured by a party of Union cavalry.

Rebels deserted the fortifications at Abbeville, Miss., and the place was occupied by the Union cavalry.

Expedition sent out from Suffolk, Va., captured the celebrated Pittsburg battery which was formerly taken from the federals, and drove the enemy across the Blackwater, at Franklin. Many of the rebels were killed and wounded, and 37 taken prisoners. Union loss small.

3. Gen. Hovey's expedition, 20,000 strong, which left Helena, Ark., on the 30th Nov., landed at Friar's Point, some 15 or 20 miles below, marched to Grenada, Miss., and took possession of the town. Rebels on the approach of the Union forces burned 15 locomotives and 100 cars.

4. Winchester, Va., captured by federals: several rebels were killed and wounded in the fight, and 145 taken prisoners.

Gen. Banks and part of his expedition sailed from New York.

5. Fight near Coffeeville, Miss. The battle lasted two hours: rebel loss, 300 killed and wounded. The federals lost 5 killed, 50 wounded, and 60 missing.

6. Rebels attacked the Union forces at Cane Hill, Ark., and were repulsed.

7. Rebels under Morgan surprised and captured a Union force near Hartville, Tenn. Rebels subsequently put to flight.

Battle of Fayetteville or Prairie Grove, Ark. Battle obstinately fought, and very sanguinary. Federal loss about 1,000 killed and wounded. In the night the rebels escaped by flight.

Capture of the California steamer "Ariel" by the C. S. steamer "Alabama." The "Ariel" was released on giving bonds for $228,000, payable 30 days after the recognition of the Confederate States.

8. President Lincoln approved the sentence on the Sioux Indians charged with murder, etc., in Minnesota, and ordered their execution.

Steamer "Lake City" destroyed by guerrillas at Concordia, Miss.

Nearly all the newspapers throughout the country were compelled to advance their prices or curtail their dimensions, in consequence of the high price of paper.

9. Concordia, on the Mississippi, burned by the Unionists in retribution for the destruction of the steamer "Lake City" by the rebels.

Sharp fighting at Lavergne, Tenn.

10. Senate bill of last session of Congress, admitting West Virginia into the Union, passed by the House of Representatives (96 *v.* 55).

Rebels appeared in force near Nashville, and drove in the Union pickets.

The Union gun-boats having been fired upon by rebel batteries in front of Port Royal, Va., shelled the town and destroyed a number of its best buildings. They also attacked the batteries, and after an engagement of two hours silenced them. Union loss, two killed and four wounded.

11. Skirmishing on the Blackwater, Va.: Union force overwhelmed by numbers and forced to retire to Suffolk, with three killed and 11 wounded.

Fredericksburg shelled, and pontoons having been laid across the river, the federals passed over in the face of a terrible fire.

Successful reconnoissance from Nashville.

Two of Gen. Banks' vessels put into Port Royal, S. C., disabled.

12. Crossing of the federal army at Fredericksburg continued, and after a few skirmishes they succeeded in taking the city. The artillery of both parties was engaged at intervals during the day, but did very little damage.

Gun-boat "Cairo" blown up by a torpedo in the Yazoo River, and sunk.

13. Battle of Fredericksburg. Fighting commenced at daybreak, but owing to a fog nothing was accomplished until afternoon, when the contest raged furiously. At night each army occupied its position. Gens. Bayard, Taylor, and Jackson

(Union) and Gens. Cobb and Gregg (rebel) were killed.

Union troops surprised and attacked the rebels at Tuscumbia, Ala., and routed them.

14. Gen. N. P. Banks arrived at New Orleans and superseded Gen. Butler in command of the Department of the Gulf.

But little fighting was done at Fredericksburg. The artillery was engaged at intervals during the day, but no point gained or damage done.

Plymouth, N. C., destroyed by rebels.

Union forces under Gen. Foster, which left Newbern after continual skirmishing on the route, advanced upon Kinston, N. C., where they met the rebels under Gen. Evans. A fight ensued, which lasted three hours, and the enemy dispersed, leaving 250 killed and wounded, 400 prisoners, together with 11 pieces of artillery, 500 stand of arms, ammunition, stores, etc., in the hands of the federals. Town entered and partially destroyed by fire.

15. Rebel salt-works at Yellville, Ark., destroyed.

The advance of Gen. Banks' expedition arrived in New Orleans.

Rebel raid to Poolesville, Md.

Firing on the rebel pickets on James Island, N. C.

16. Fredericksburg, Va., evacuated by the federals during last night, and the pontoons over the river removed before the enemy was aware of the movement. The Union army occupied Falmouth.

Major-Gen. Banks assumed command of the Department of the Gulf, and Gen. Butler issued a farewell address to the army.

Gen. Burnside wrote his celebrated letter assuming

the responsibility of the failure before Fredericksburg.

17. A detachment of the Banks' expedition sent up the Mississippi River from New Orleans, and the troops under Gen. Grover entered and took possession of Baton Rouge, the capital of Louisiana.

18. Rebels captured a small body of Union men at Lexington, Tenn. In the fight the federals lost seven killed, 10 wounded, and 110 prisoners, and rebels 35 killed and wounded.

The expedition under Gen. Foster returned to Newbern, N. C. It was absent eight days, during which it lost between 200 and 300 men. It fought four battles, and had numerous skirmishes along the Neuse River and railroad track. The battles of Goldsboro' and Whitehall were splendid victories.

19. Holly Springs, Miss., retaken by the rebels, and the whole garrison made prisoners. About 200 federals were killed and wounded, and about half a million dollars' worth of government stores burned. The rebels also burned 4,000 bales of cotton.

20. Rebels attacked the Union force at Davies' Mills, near Grand Junction, Tenn., but were driven off, leaving 20 dead and 30 wounded on the field.

A body of Confederate cavalry made a raid on the railroad near Jackson, Tenn., and fired into a passing train. Subsequently they burned a long tresselwork and tore up the track for a considerable distance.

21. A body of cavalry, 1,000 strong, under Gen. Carter, from London, Ky., set out on an expedition for the purpose of destroying two important railroad

bridges in East Tennessee. They succeeded in their object, and, besides, destroyed several locomotives and cars, and captured 500 prisoners and 700 stand of arms.

22. Secretaries Seward and Chase sent in their resignations to the President. They were not accepted, and the said Secretaries resumed their positions.

President Lincoln issued an address to the Army of the Potomac in regard to the recent occurrences at Fredericksburg.

23. President Davis issued a retaliatory proclamation denouncing the course of Gen. Butler in New Orleans, and dooming him and all his officers to death by the halter whenever caught; and further ordered that no commissioned officer of the United States should be released or parolled before exchanged until Gen. Butler was punished.

Winchester, Va., occupied by the Union forces.

The Confederates, 4,000 strong, attacked a portion of Gen. Sigel's command at Dumfries, Va., and after a heavy skirmish were repulsed.

24. Severe skirmish on the Blackwater.

25. Glasgow, Ky., occupied by the rebels.

Rebels reported to have re-entered Eastern Kentucky through Pound Gap.

26. Thirty-eight Sioux Indians, condemned as participators in the late disturbances in Minnesota, were executed by hanging at Mankato, Minn.

Gen. Sherman debarked his forces on the left bank of the Yazoo River, 10 miles above its mouth, and forming in line of battle, advanced on Vicksburg.

Gen. Rosecrans moved his army from Nashville in the direction of Murfreesboro, Tenn., and on the 29th came in sight of the enemy's works.

27. Steamship "Ariel" arrived at New York and reported her capture by the "Alabama."

A company of Union cavalry surprised and captured by the Confederates at Occoquan, Va.

A body of 350 Confederates surprised at Elk Fork, Campbell Co., Ky., by two companies of Kentucky cavalry. In the fight 17 were killed and wounded and 57 captured. and all their camp equipage was destroyed.

The Union forces attacked the advance works of the rebels extending six miles back of Vicksburg. Meanwhile the gun-boats attacked the batteries on Haines' Bluff. A portion of the expedition was also sent to destroy the Vicksburg and Shreveport Railroad, in order to prevent the arrival of reinforcements.

28. Capitol at Baton Rouge, La., destroyed by fire.

Battle at Van Buren, Ark.: after a short engagement the rebels were driven across the river. Two steamers and 100 prisoners were captured by the federals, and also large quantities of corn, camp equipage, horses, etc.

Union troops evacuated New Madrid.

Unsuccessful attempts of the rebel Gen. Stuart to capture the dépôt of stores at Fairfax Station, Va.

After a stubborn contest yesterday and to-day, the Confederates were driven from their first and second lines of defense, and the federals advanced to within two and a half miles of Vicksburg.

29. The Confederates having been heavily reinforced from Grenada and along the railroad, attacked the federals with their full force, and succeeded in driving them back to their first line of defense. In the attack on Vicksburg, Gen. Sherman was to

have had the co-operation of Gen. Grant, but that general had been compelled to fall back from Holly Springs, which not only made co-operation impossible, but had given the enemy the opportunity of bringing in reinforcements. The consequence was that the federals had to withdraw from the contest.

Skirmishing near Stewart's Creek, in which the federals lost 70 killed and wounded, but took upward of 100 prisoners.

30. Skirmishing near Stewart's Creek continued, without apparent result.

31. The Bill admitting West Virginia as a State of the Union signed by the President.

The "Monitor" (iron steamer) sunk at sea, south of Cape Hatteras. Two officers and 38 men lost.

At daybreak the fight before Murfreesboro was renewed with great fury. After desperate fighting, with heavy losses, a portion of the federal force was driven back, and at night was four miles from the position occupied in the morning, with the loss of 26 guns.

January, 1863.

1. Battle of Galveston: commenced at 5 A.M. by a fight between the U. S. blockading squadron and the rebel batteries at Virginia Point. About 6 A.M. several rebel steamers protected by cotton bales joined in the fight, and captured the U. S. steamer "Harriet Lane," which had become disabled by a collision. The U. S. steamer "Westfield" was blown up by her commander and all hands per-

ished, and subsequently the rebels entered the city and massacred the small garrison stationed there.

Fight before Murfreesboro continued. The battle was renewed with varying success and with fearful loss on both sides until the 4th, when the Confederates retreated. The entire loss by the federals, from the first set-to near Stewart's Creek on the 29th to the 4th inst., was estimated at not less than 1,500 killed, 6,000 wounded, and 4,000 prisoners. The Confederate loss, from their intrenched position, was not so large.

Gen. Sherman sent in a flag of truce asking leave of the rebels to bury his dead; and on the 2d the federal expedition withdrew from the vicinity of Vicksburg.

Gen. Sherman was superseded by Gen. McClernand.

Gen. Sullivan with a force of 6,000 men attacked the rebels under Forest, near Lexington, Tenn., and after an engagement lasting all day defeated them, with very heavy loss in men and guns.

Guerrillas under Morgan attacked and repulsed by the federal troops under Col. Haskins at Lebanon, Ky.

President Lincoln issued his emancipation proclamation.

Public debt of the United States:

Loan of 1842 in course of payment	$2,383,364 11
Loan of 1847	9,415,250 00
Loan of 1848	8,908,341 80
Loan of 1858	20,000,000 00
Loan of 1860	7,022,000 00
Loan of 1861, act of Feb. 8, 1860	10,415,000 00
Loan of 1861, act of July 18, 1861	50,002,000 00
Loan of 1862, five-twenty 6 per cent	25,050,850 00
Texas indemnity	3,461,000 00
Oregon war debt	1,026,600 00

Texas debt	$112,092 59
Old funded and unfunded debt	114,115 48
Treasury notes under acts for 1857	104,561 64
Treasury notes under acts subsequent	2,750,350 00
Treasury notes 7-30 per cent. interest	139,998,000 00
Temporary deposits at 4 per cent.	38,458,008 00
Temporary deposits at 5 per cent.	41,777,638 00
U. S. notes receivable for customs	14,913,315 25
U. S. notes legal tender	223,108,000 00
Postal currency less than one dollar	6,844,936 00
Certificates of indebtedness, 6 per cent.	110,321,241 65
Requisitions on the Treasury for soldiers' pay and other creditors, due but not paid	59,117,597 46
Total funded and unfunded debt	$783,804,252 64

Public debt of the Confederate States:

BONDS AND STOCKS.

Under act of Feb. 28, 1861		$14,887,000
" " May 16, 1861		6,414,300
" " Aug. 19, 1861		67,585,100
" " Dec. 24, 1861—		
Deposit certificates	$89,055,870	
" " redeemed	12,516,400—	66,488,470
Total bonds and stocks		$145,476,870

TREASURY NOTES.

3.65 per cent. notes	$992,000	
Two years' notes	10,919,025	
General currency	272,022,467	
7.30 per cent. notes	120,480,000	
$1 and $2 notes	6,216,200—	410,629,692
Total funded and floating debt		$556,105,062

APPENDIX,

CONTAINING THE SEVERAL ORDINANCES OF SECESSION ADOPTED BY THE REBEL SECEDED STATES; THE MORE IMPORTANT PROCLAMATIONS OF THE PRESIDENT OF THE UNITED STATES, AND OTHER DOCUMENTS ILLUSTRATIVE OF THE PERIOD EMBRACED IN THE CHRONOLOGICAL HISTORY OF THE GREAT REBELLION.

ORDINANCES OF SECESSION.

Alabama Ordinance.

(Passed in secret session of convention at Montgomery, 11th January, 1861, by a vote of 61 *ayes* to 39 *nays*.)

Whereas the election of Abraham Lincoln and Hannibal Hamlin to the offices of President and Vice-President of the United States of America by a sectional party, avowedly hostile to the domestic institutions and to the peace and security of the people of the State of Alabama, preceded by many and dangerous infractions of the Constitution of the United States by many of the States and people of the Northern section, is a political wrong of so insulting and menacing a character as to justify the people of the State of Alabama in the adoption of prompt and decided measures for their future peace and security: Therefore,

Be it declared and ordained by the people of the State of Alabama, in convention assembled, That the State of Alabama now withdraws, and is hereby withdrawn, from the Union known as "the United States of America," and henceforth ceases to be one of said United States, and is, and of right ought to be, a sovereign and independent State.

SEC. 2. *Be it further declared and ordained by the people of the State of Alabama, in convention assembled,* That all the powers over the territory of said State, and over the people thereof, heretofore delegated to the Government of the United States of America be, and they are hereby, withdrawn from said Government, and are hereby resumed and vested in the people of the State of Alabama.

And as it is the desire and purpose of the State of Alabama to meet the slaveholding States of the South who may approve such purpose, in order to frame a provisional as well as permanent government, upon the principles of the Constitution of the United States,

Be it resolved by the people of Alabama, in convention assembled, That the people of the States of Delaware, Maryland, Virginia, North Carolina, South Carolina, Florida, Georgia, Mississippi, Louisiana, Texas, Arkansas, Tennessee, Kentucky, and Missouri, be, and are hereby, invited to meet the people of the State of Alabama, by their delegates, in convention, on the 4th day of February, A.D. 1861, at the city of Montgomery, in the State of Alabama, for the purpose of consulting with each other as to the most effectual mode of securing concerted and harmonious action in whatever measures may be deemed most desirable for our common peace and security.

And be it further resolved, That the president of this convention be, and is hereby, instructed to transmit forthwith a copy of the foregoing preamble, ordinance, and resolution, to the Governors of the several States named in said resolution.

Arkansas Ordinance.

(Passed in convention at Little Rock, 6th May, 1861, by a vote of 69 *ayes* to 1 *nay*.)

Whereas, in addition to the well-founded causes of complaint set forth by this convention, in resolutions adopted on the 11th March, A.D. 1861, against the sectional party now in power at Washington City, headed by Abraham Lincoln, he has, in the face of resolutions passed by this convention, pledging the State of Arkansas to resist to the last extremity any attempt on the part of such power to coerce any State that seceded from the old Union, proclaimed to the world that war should be waged against such States until they should be compelled to submit to their rule, and large forces to accomplish this have by this same power been called out, and are now being marshaled to carry out this inhuman design, and to longer submit to such rule or remain in the old Union of the United States would be disgraceful and ruinous to the State of Arkansas:

Therefore, we, the people of the State of Arkansas, in convention assembled, do hereby declare and ordain, and it is hereby declared and ordained, that the "ordinance and acceptance of compact," passed and approved by the General Assembly of the State of Arkansas, on the 18th day of October, A.D. 1836, whereby it was by said General Assembly ordained that, by virtue of the authority vested in said General Assembly, by the provisions of the ordinance adopted by the convention of delegates assembled at Little Rock, for the purpose of forming a constitution and system of government for said State, the propositions set forth in "an act supplementary to an act entitled an act for the admission of the State of Arkansas into the Union, and to provide for the due execution of the laws of the United States within the same, and for other purposes, were freely accepted, ratified, and irrevocably confirmed articles of compact and union between the State of Arkansas and the United States," and all other laws and every other law and ordinance, whereby the State of Arkansas became a member of the Federal Union be, and the same are hereby in all respects and for every purpose herewith consistent repealed, abrogated, and fully set aside; and the union now subsisting between the State of Arkansas and the other States, under the name of the United States of America, is hereby forever dissolved.

And we do further hereby declare and ordain, that the State of Arkansas hereby resumes to herself all rights and powers heretofore delegated to the Government of the United States of America—that her citizens are absolved from all allegiance to said Government of the United States, and that she is in full possession and exercise of all the rights and sovereignty which appertain to a free and independent State.

We do further ordain and declare, that all rights acquired and vested under the Constitution of the United States of America, or of any act or acts of Congress, or treaty, or under any law of this State, and not incompatible with this ordinance, shall remain in full force and effect, in nowise altered or impaired, and have the same effect as if this ordinance had not been passed.

Florida Ordinance.

(Passed in convention at Tallahassee, 7th January, 1861, by a vote of 62 *ayes* to 7 *nays*.)

Whereas, All hope of preserving the Union upon terms consistent with the safety and honor of the slaveholding States has been fully dissipated by the recent indications of the strength of the anti-slavery sentiment of the free States; therefore,

Be it enacted by the people of Florida, in convention assembled, That it is undoubtedly the right of the several States of the Union, at such time and for such cause as in the opinion of the people of such States, acting in their sovereign capacity, may be just and proper, to withdraw from the Union, and, in the opinion of this convention, the existing causes are such as to compel Florida to proceed to exercise this right.

We, the people of the State of Florida, in convention assembled, do solemnly ordain, publish, and declare that the State of Florida hereby withdraws herself from the Confederacy of States existing under the name of the United States of America, and from the existing Government of the said States; and that all political connection between her and the Government of said States ought to be, and the same is hereby totally annulled, and said Union of States dissolved; and the

State of Florida is hereby declared a sovereign and independent nation; and that all ordinances heretofore adopted, in so far as they create or recognize said Union, are rescinded; and all laws, or parts of laws, in force in this State, in so far as they recognize or assent to said Union, be, and they are hereby repealed.

Georgia Ordinance.

(Passed in convention at Milledgeville, 19th January, 1861, by a vote of 208 *ayes* to 89 *nays*.)

We, the people of the State of Georgia, in convention assembled, do declare and ordain, and it is hereby declared and ordained, that the ordinance adopted by the people of Georgia in convention in the year 1788, whereby the Constitution of the United States was assented to, ratified, and adopted, and also all acts and parts of acts of the General Assembly ratifying and adopting the amendments to the said Constitution, are hereby repealed, rescinded, and abrogated; and we do further declare and ordain, that the Union now subsisting between the State of Georgia and other States, under the name of the United States of America, is hereby dissolved; and that the State of Georgia is in full possession and exercise of all those rights of sovereignty which belong and appertain to a free and independent State.

Louisiana Ordinance.

(Passed in convention at Baton Rouge, 26th January, 1861, by a vote of 113 *ayes* to 17 *nays*.)

We, the people of the State of Louisiana, in convention assembled, do declare and ordain, and it is hereby declared and ordained, that the ordinance passed by us in convention on the 22d day of November, in the year 1811, whereby the Constitution of the United States of America, and the amendments of said Constitution, were adopted, and all laws and ordinances by which the State of Louisiana became a member of the Federal Union, be, and the same are hereby, repealed and abrogated; and that the union now subsisting between Louisiana and other States, under the name of the "United States of America," is hereby dissolved.

We do further declare and ordain, that the State of Louisiana hereby resumes all rights and powers heretofore delegated to the Government of the United States of America; that her citizens are absolved from all allegiance to said Government: and that she is in full possession and exercise of all those rights of sovereignty which appertain to a free and independent State.

We do further declare and ordain, that all rights acquired and vested under the Constitution of the United States, or any act of Congress, or treaty, or under any law of this State and not incompatible with this ordinance, shall remain in force, and have the same effect as if this ordinance had not been passed.

Mississippi Ordinance.

(Passed in convention at Jackson, 9th January, 1861, by a vote of 84 *ayes* to 15 *nays*.)

The people of Mississippi, in convention assembled, do ordain and declare, and it is hereby ordained and declared, as follows, to wit:

SEC. 1. That all the laws and ordinances by which the said State of Mississippi became a member of the Federal Union of the United States of America be, and the same are hereby repealed, and that all obligations on the part of the said State, or the people thereof, be withdrawn, and that the said State does hereby resume all the rights, functions, and powers which by any of the said laws and ordinances were conveyed to the Government of the said United States, and is absolved from all the obligations, restraints, and duties incurred to the said Federal Union, and shall henceforth be a free, sovereign, and independent State.

SEC. 2. That so much of the first section of the seventh article of the Constitution of this State, as requires members of the Legislature and all officers, both legislative and judicial, to take an oath to support the Constitution of the United States be, and the same is, hereby abrogated and annulled.

SEC. 3. That all rights acquired and vested under the Constitution of the United States, or under any act of Congress passed in pursuance thereof, or any law of this State, and not incompatible with this ordinance, shall remain in force, and have the same effect as if the ordinance had not been passed.

SEC. 4. That the people of the State of Mississippi hereby consent to form a Federal Union with such of the States as have seceded or may secede from the Union of the United States of America, upon the basis of the present Constitution of the United States, except such parts thereof as embrace other portions than such seceding States.

North Carolina Ordinance.

(Passed in convention at Raleigh, 21st May, 1861, by a unanimous vote.)

We, the people of the State of North Carolina, in convention assembled, do declare and ordain, and it is hereby declared and ordained, that the ordinance adopted by the State of North Carolina, in the convention of 1789, whereby the Constitution of the United States was ratified and adopted, and also all acts and parts of acts of the General Assembly, ratifying and adopting amendments to the said Constitution, are hereby repealed, rescinded, and abrogated.

We do further declare and ordain that the Union now subsisting between the State of North Carolina and the other States, under the title of the United States of America, is hereby dissolved, and that the State of North Carolina is in the full possession and exercise of all those rights of sovereignty which belong and appertain to a free and independent State.

South Carolina Ordinance.*

(Passed in convention at Charleston, 20th December, 1860, by a unanimous vote.)

We, the people of the State of South Carolina, in convention assembled, do declare and ordain, and it

---

* On the 24th December the convention adopted the following "Declaration of Independence:"

The State of South Carolina, having determined to resume her separate and equal place among nations, deems it due to herself, to the remaining United States of America, and to the nations of the world, that she should declare the causes which have led to this act.

In the year 1765, that portion of the British Empire embracing Great Britain undertook to make laws for the government of that portion composed of the thirteen American Colonies. A struggle for the right of self-government ensued, which resulted, on the 4th of July, 1776, in a Declaration by the Colonies, "that they are, and of right ought to be, free and independent States, and that, as free and independent States, they have full power to levy war, to conclude peace, contract alliances, establish commerce, and to do all other acts and things which independent States may of right do."

They further solemnly declared, that whenever any "form of government becomes destructive of the ends for which it is established, it is the right of the people to alter or abolish it, and to institute a new government." Deeming the government of Great Britain to have become destructive of these ends, they declared that the Colonies "are absolved from all allegiance to the British crown, and that all political connection between them and the States of Great Britain is, and ought to be, totally dissolved."

In pursuance of this Declaration of Independence, each of the thirteen States proceeded to exercise its separate sovereignty, adopted for itself a constitution, and appointed officers for the administration of government in all its departments—legislative, executive, and judicial. For purposes of defense, they united their arms and their counsels; and in 1778 they entered into a league, known as the articles of confederation, whereby they agreed to intrust the administration of their external relations to a common agent, known as the Congress of the United States, expressly declaring, in the first article, "that each State retains its sovereignty, freedom, and independence, and every power, jurisdiction, and right which is not, by this confederation, expressly delegated to the United States in Congress assembled."

Under this confederation the war of the Revolution was carried on, and on the 3d of September, 1783, the contest ended, and a definitive treaty was signed by Great Britain, in which she acknowledged the independence of the Colonies in the following terms:

"ARTICLE 1.—His Britannic Majesty acknowledges the said United States, viz.: New Hampshire, Massachusetts Bay, Rhode Island and Providence Plantations, Connecticut, New York, New Jersey, Pennsylvania, Delaware, Maryland, Virginia, North Carolina, South Carolina, is hereby declared and ordained, that the ordinance adopted by us in convention on the 23d day of May, in

---

and Georgia, to be free, sovereign, and independent States; that he treats with them as such; and for himself, his heirs and successors, relinquishes all claim to the government, proprietary and territorial rights of the same and every part thereof."

Thus was established the two great principles asserted by the Colonies, namely, the right of a State to govern itself, and the right of a people to abolish a government when it becomes destructive of the ends for which it was instituted. And concurrent with the establishment of these principles was the fact, that each colony became and was recognized by the mother country as a free, sovereign, and independent State.

In 1787, Deputies were appointed by the States to revise the articles of confederation, and on the 17th September, 1787, these Deputies recommended for the adoption of the States the articles of union known as the Constitution of the United States.

The parties to whom this Constitution was submitted were the several sovereign States; they were to agree or disagree, and when nine of them agreed the compact was to take effect among those concurring; and the general government, as the common agent, was then to be invested with their authority.

If only nine of the thirteen States had concurred, the other four would have remained as they then were—separate, sovereign States, independent of any of the provisions of the Constitution. In fact, two of the States did not accede to the Constitution until long after it had gone into operation among the other eleven; and during that interval they exercised the functions of an independent nation.

By this Constitution certain duties were charged on the several States, and the exercise of certain of their powers restrained, which necessarily implied their continued existence as sovereign States. But to remove all doubt, an amendment was added, which declared that the powers not delegated to the United States by the Constitution, nor prohibited by it to the States, are reserved to the States respectively, or to the people. On 23d May, 1788, South Carolina, by a convention of her people, passed an ordinance assenting to this Constitution, and afterward altered her own constitution to conform herself to the obligations she had undertaken.

Thus was established, by compact between the States, a government, with defined objects and powers, limited to the express words of the grant, and to so much more only as was necessary to execute the power granted. This limitation left the whole remaining mass of power subject to the clause reserving it to the States or to the people, and rendered unnecessary any specification of reserved rights.

We hold that the government thus established is subject to the two great principles asserted in the Declaration of Independence, and we hold further that the mode of its formation subjects it to a third fundamental principle, namely, the law of compact. We maintain that, in every compact between two or more parties, the obligation is mutual—that the failure of one of the contracting parties to perform a material part of the agreement entirely releases the obligation of the

the year of our Lord 1788, whereby the Constitution of the United States was ratified, and also all acts and

---

other, and that, where no arbiter is provided, each party is remitted to his own judgment to determine the fact of failure with all its consequences.

In the present case that fact is established with certainty. We assert that fifteen of the States have deliberately refused for years past to fulfill their constitutional obligations, and we refer to their own statutes for the proof.

The Constitution of the United States, in its 4th article, provides as follows:

"No person held to service or labor in one State, under the laws thereof, escaping into another, shall, in consequence of any law or regulation therein, be discharged from such service or labor, but shall be delivered up on claim of the party to whom such service or labor may be due."

This stipulation was so material to the compact, that without it that compact would not have been made. The greater number of the contracting parties held slaves, and the State of Virginia had previously declared her estimate of its value by making it the condition of her cession of the territory which now compose the States north of the Ohio River.

The same article of the Constitution stipulates also for the rendition by the several States of fugitives from justice from the other States.

The general government, as the common agent, passed laws to carry into effect these stipulations of the States. For many years these laws were executed. But an increasing hostility on the part of the Northern States to the institution of slavery has led to a disregard of their obligations, and the laws of the general government have ceased to effect the objects of the Constitution. The States of Maine, New Hampshire, Vermont, Massachusetts, Connecticut, Rhode Island, New York, Pennsylvania, Illinois, Indiana, Ohio, Michigan, Wisconsin, and Iowa have enacted laws which either nullify the acts of Congress or render useless any attempt to execute them. In many of these States the fugitive is discharged from the service or labor claimed, and in none of them has the State government complied with the stipulation made in the Constitution. The State of New Jersey, at an early day, passed a law for the rendition of fugitive slaves, in conformity with her constitutional undertaking; but the current of anti-slavery feeling has led her more recently to enact laws which render inoperative the remedies provided by her own law and the laws of Congress. In the State of New York even the right of transit for a slave has been denied by her tribunals, and the States of Ohio and Iowa have refused to surrender to justice fugitives charged with murder and with inciting servile insurrection in the State of Virginia. Thus the constitutional compact has been deliberately broken and disregarded by the nonslaveholding States, and the consequence follows that South Carolina is released from its obligations.

The ends for which the Constitution was framed are declared by itself to be "to form a more perfect union, establish justice, insure domestic tranquillity, provide for the common defense, protect the parts of acts of the General Assembly of the State ratifying amendments of the said Constitution, are

---

general welfare, and secure the blessings of liberty to ourselves and our posterity."

These ends it endeavored to accomplish by a federal government, in which each State was recognized as an equal, and had separate control over its own institutions. The right of property in slaves was recognized by giving to free persons distinct political rights; by giving them the right to represent, and burdening them with direct taxes for three fifths of their slaves; by authorizing the importation of slaves for twenty years, and by stipulating for the rendition of fugitives from labor.

We affirm that these ends, for which this government was instituted, have been defeated, and the government itself has been made destructive of them by the action of the non-slaveholding States. These States have assumed the right of deciding upon the propriety of our domestic institutions, and have denied the rights of property established in fifteen of the States and recognized by the Constitution; they have denounced as sinful the institution of slavery; they have permitted the open establishment among them of societies whose avowed object is to disturb the peace and to eloin the property of the citizens of other States. They have encouraged and assisted thousands of our slaves to leave their homes, and those who remain have been incited by emissaries, books, and pictures to servile insurrection.

For twenty-five years this agitation has been steadily increasing, until it has now secured to its aid the power of the common government. Observing the forms of the Constitution, a sectional party has found within that article establishing the executive department the means of subverting the Constitution itself. A geographical line has been drawn across the Union, and all the States north of that line have united in the election of a man to the high office of President of the United States, whose opinions and purposes are hostile to slavery. He is to be intrusted with the administration of the common government, because he has declared that that "government can not endure permanently half slave, half free," and that the public mind must rest in the belief that slavery is in the course of ultimate extinction.

This sectional combination for the subversion of the Constitution has been aided in some of the States by elevating to citizenship persons who, by the supreme law of the land, are incapable of becoming citizens, and their votes have been used to inaugurate a new policy hostile to the South, and destructive of its peace and safety.

On the 4th March next, this party will take possession of the government. It has announced that the South shall be excluded from the common territory; that the judicial tribunals shall be made sectional, and that a war must be waged against slavery until it shall cease throughout the United States.

The guaranties of the Constitution will then no longer exist; the equal rights of the States will be lost. The slaveholding States will no longer have the power of self-government or self-protection, and the federal government will have become their enemies.

Sectional interest and animosity will deepen the irritation, and all hereby repealed, and the Union now subsisting between South Carolina and other States, under the name of "The United States of America," is hereby dissolved.

Tennessee Declaration of Independence and Ordinance.*

(Passed the Legislature at Nashville, 6th May, 1861, by a vote in the Senate of 20 *ayes* to 4 *nays*, and in the House of Representatives by a vote of 46 *ayes* and 21 *nays*, but subject to acceptance or rejection by vote of the people.)

1st. We, the people of the State of Tennessee, waiving an expression of opinion as to the abstract doctrine of secession, but asserting the right as a free and independent people to alter, reform, or abolish our form of government in such manner as we think proper, do ordain and declare that all the laws and ordinances by which the State of Tennessee became a member of the Federal Union of the United States of America, are hereby abrogated and annulled, and that all obligations

---

hope of remedy is rendered vain by the fact that public opinion at the North has invested a great political error with the sanctions of a more erroneous religious belief.

We, therefore, the people of South Carolina, by our delegates in convention assembled, appealing to the Supreme Judge of the world for the rectitude of our intentions, have solemnly declared that the union heretofore existing between this State and the other States of North America is dissolved, and that the State of South Carolina has resumed her position among the nations of the world as a free, sovereign, and independent State, with full power to levy war, conclude peace, contract alliances, establish commerce, and to do all other acts and things which independent States may of right do.

And, for the support of this declaration, with a firm reliance on the protection of Divine Providence, we mutually pledge to each other our lives, our fortunes, and our sacred honor.

* The aggregate votes in the several divisions of the State taken on the 8th June, 1861, was as follows:

Divisions of State.	Separation Votes.	No separation Votes.	Majority for "Separation."	Majority for "No separt."
East Tennessee	14,780	32,923	—	18,143
Middle Tennessee	58,265	8,198	50,067	—
West Tennessee	29,127	6,116	23,010	—
Military camps	2,741	—	2,741	—
Total	104,913	47,238	57,675	—

on our part be withdrawn therefrom; and we do hereby resume all the rights, functions, and powers which by any of said laws and ordinances were conveyed to the Government of the United States, and absolve ourselves from all the obligations, restraints, and duties incurred thereto; and do hereby henceforth become a free, sovereign, and independent State.

2d. We furthermore declare and ordain, that Article 10, Sections 1 and 2 of the Constitution of the State of Tennessee, which requires members of the General Assembly, and all officers, civil and military, to take an oath to support the Constitution of the United States, be, and the same are hereby abrogated and annulled, and all parts of the Constitution of the State of Tennessee, making citizenship of the United States a qualification for office, and recognizing the Constitution of the United States as the supreme law of this State, are in like manner abrogated and annulled.

3d. We furthermore ordain and declare that all rights acquired and vested under the Constitution of the United States, or under any act of Congress passed in pursuance thereof, or under any laws of this State, and not incompatible with this ordinance, shall remain in force and have the same effect as if this ordinance had not been passed.

Texas Ordinance.*

(Passed in convention at Houston, 1st February, 1861, by a vote of 166 *ayes* to 7 *nays*.)

Sec. 1. Whereas the Federal Government has failed to accomplish the purposes of the compact of union between these States, in giving protection either to the persons of our people upon an exposed frontier, or to the property of our citizens; and whereas the action of the Northern States is violative of the compact be-

* The vote in 89 counties of the State was: for secession 34,794 and against 11,235—majority for secession 23,559. The vote for President in November, 1860, was 62,986, showing that large numbers either declined or had not the opportunity to vote on the question.

tween the States and the guarantees of the Constitution; and whereas the recent developments in Federal affairs make it evident that the power of the Federal Government is sought to be made a weapon with which to strike down the interests and property of the people of Texas and her sister slaveholding States, instead of permitting it to be, as was intended—our shield against outrage and aggression—therefore, "We, the people of the State of Texas, by delegates in the convention assembled, do declare and ordain that the ordinance adopted by our convention of delegates on the fourth (4th) day of July, A.D. 1845, and afterward ratified by us, under which the Republic of Texas was admitted into the Union with other States, and became a party to the compact styled 'The Constitution of the United States of America,' be, and is hereby repealed and annulled."

That all the powers which, by the said compact, were delegated by Texas to the Federal Government are resumed. That Texas is of right absolved from all restraints and obligations incurred by said compact, and is a separate sovereign State, and that her citizens and people are absolved from all allegiance to the United States or the Government thereof.

SEC. 2. The ordinance shall be submitted to the people of Texas for their ratification or rejection, by the qualified voters, on the 23d day of February, 1861; and unless rejected by a majority of the votes cast, shall take effect and be in force on and after the 2d day of March, A.D. 1861. Provided that in the representative district of El Paso said election may be held on the 18th day of February, 1861.

Virginia Ordinance.

(Passed in convention at Richmond, 17th April, 1861, by a vote of 88 *ayes* to 55 *nays*.)

The people of Virginia, in the ratification of the Constitution of the United States of America, adopted by them in convention, on the 25th day of June, in the year of our Lord 1788, having declared that the powers granted under the said Constitution were derived from the people of the United States, and might be resumed whensoever the same should be perverted to their injury and oppression, and the Federal Government having perverted said powers, not only to the injury of the people of Virginia, but to the oppression of the Southern slaveholding States;

Now, therefore, we, the people of Virginia, do declare and ordain, that the ordinance adopted by the people of this State in convention on the 25th day of June, in the year of our Lord 1788, whereby the Constitution of the United States of America was ratified, and all acts of the General Assembly of this State ratifying or adopting amendments to said Constitution, are hereby repealed and abrogated; that the union between the State of Virginia and the other States under the Constitution aforesaid is hereby dissolved, and that the State of Virginia is in the full possession and exercise of all the rights of sovereignty which belong and appertain to a free and independent State. And they do further declare that said Constitution of the United States of America is no longer binding on any of the citizens of this State.

This ordinance shall take effect and be an act of this day, when ratified by a majority of the votes of the people of this State, cast at a poll to be taken thereon, on the fourth Thursday in May next, in pursuance of a schedule hereafter to be enacted.

☞ The result of the popular vote on the question of ratifying the ordinance was : for ratification 125,950 and for rejection 20,373—majority for ratification 105,577. The vote at the Presidential election in November was 167,223.

PROCLAMATIONS OF THE PRESIDENT OF THE UNITED STATES.

Proclamation of the 15th April, 1861, calling for 75,000 militia and summoning Congress to meet at Washington on the 4th July, 1861 :

Whereas the laws of the United States have been for some time past and now are opposed, and the execution thereof obstructed, in the States of South Carolina, Georgia, Alabama, Florida, Mississippi, Louisiana, and Texas, by combinations too powerful to be suppressed by the ordinary course of judicial proceedings, or by the powers vested in the marshals by law:

Now, therefore, I, Abraham Lincoln, President of the United States, in virtue of the power in me vested by the Constitution and the laws, have thought fit to call forth, and hereby do call forth the militia of the several States of the Union, to the aggregate number of seventy-five thousand, in order to suppress said combinations, and to cause the laws to be duly executed.

The details for this object will be immediately communicated to the State authorities through the War Department.

I appeal to all loyal citizens to favor, facilitate, and aid this effort to maintain the honor, the integrity, and the existence of our National Union, and the perpetuity of popular government, and to redress wrongs already long enough endured.

I deem it proper to say that the first service assigned to the forces called forth will probably be to repossess the forts, places, and property which have been seized from the Union; and in every event the utmost care will be observed, consistently with the objects aforesaid, to avoid any devastation, any destruction of or interference with property, or any disturbance of peaceful citizens in any part of the country.

And I hereby command the persons composing the combinations aforesaid to disperse and retire peaceably to their respective abodes within twenty days from this date.

Deeming that the present condition of public affairs presents an extraordinary occasion, I do hereby, in virtue of the power in me vested by the Constitution, convene both Houses of Congress.

Senators and Representatives are therefore summoned to assemble at their respective Chambers, at 12 o'clock, noon, on Thursday, the fourth day of July next, then and there to consider and determine such measures as, in their wisdom, the public safety and interest may seem to demand.

Proclamation of 19th April, 1861, declaring the blockade of the ports of South Carolina, Georgia, Alabama, Florida, Mississippi, Louisiana, and Texas:

Whereas an insurrection against the Government of the United States has broken out in the States of South Carolina, Georgia, Alabama, Florida, Mississippi, Louisiana, and Texas, and the laws of the United States for the collection of the revenue can not be effectually executed therein conformably to that provision of the Constitution which requires duties to be uniform throughout the United States:

And whereas a combination of persons, engaged in such insurrection, have threatened to grant pretended letters of marque to authorize the bearers thereof to commit assault on the lives, vessels, and property of good citizens of the country lawfully engaged in commerce on the high seas, and in waters of the United States:

And whereas an Executive Proclamation has been already issued, requiring the persons engaged in these disorderly proceedings to desist therefrom, calling out a militia force for the purpose of repressing the same, and convening Congress in extraordinary session to deliberate and determine thereon:

Now, therefore, I, Abraham Lincoln, President of the United States, with a view to the same purposes before mentioned, and to the protection of the public peace, and the lives and property of quiet and orderly citizens pursuing their lawful occupations, until Congress shall have assembled and deliberated on the said unlawful proceedings, or until the same shall have ceased, have further deemed it advisable to set on foot a blockade of the ports within the States aforesaid, in pursuance of the laws of the United States and of the laws of nations in such case provided. For this purpose a competent force will be posted so as to prevent entrance and exit of vessels from the ports aforesaid. If, therefore, with a view to violate such blockade, a vessel shall approach, or shall attempt to leave any of the said ports, she will be duly warned by the commander of one of the blockading vessels, who will indorse on her register the fact and date of such warning, and if the same vessel shall again attempt to enter or leave the blockaded port, she will be captured and sent to the nearest convenient port, for such proceedings against her and her cargo as prize as may be deemed advisable.

And I hereby proclaim and declare that if any person, under the pretended authority of the said States, or under any other pretense, shall molest a vessel of the United States, or the persons or cargo on board of her, such person will be held amenable to the laws of the United States for the prevention and punishment of piracy.

Proclamation of 16th August, 1861, suspending commercial intercourse with States in rebellion :

Whereas, on the 15th day of April, 1861, the President of the United States, in view of an insurrection against the Laws, Constitution, and Government of the United States, which had broken out within the States of South Carolina, Georgia, Alabama, Florida, Mississippi, Louisiana, and Texas, and in pursuance of the provisions of the act entitled "An act to provide for calling forth the militia to execute the laws of the

Union, suppress insurrections, and repel invasions, and to repeal the act now in force for that purpose," approved February 28, 1795, did call forth the militia to suppress said insurrection, and to cause the laws of the Union to be duly executed, and the insurgents have failed to disperse by the time directed by the President; and, whereas, such insurrection has since broken out, and yet exists, within the States of Virginia, North Carolina, Tennessee, and Arkansas; and, whereas, the insurgents in all the said States claim to act under the authority thereof, and such claim is not disclaimed or repudiated by the persons exercising the functions of government in such State or States, or in the part or parts thereof in which such combinations exist, nor has such insurrection been suppressed by said States:

Now, therefore, I, Abraham Lincoln, President of the United States, in pursuance of an act of Congress, approved July 13, 1861, do hereby declare that the inhabitants of the said States of Georgia, South Carolina, Virginia, North Carolina, Tennessee, Alabama, Louisiana, Texas, Arkansas, Mississippi, and Florida (except the inhabitants of that part of the State of Virginia lying west of the Alleghany Mountains, and of such other parts of that State and the other States hereinbefore named as may maintain a loyal adhesion to the Union and the Constitution, or may be from time to time occupied and controlled by forces of the United States engaged in the dispersion of said insurgents), are in a state of insurrection against the United States, and that all commercial intercourse between the same and the inhabitants thereof, with the exceptions aforesaid, and the citizens of other States and other parts of the United States is unlawful, and will remain unlawful until such insurrection shall cease or has been suppressed; that all goods and chattels, wares and merchandise, coming from any of said States, with the exceptions aforesaid, into other parts of the United States, without the special license and permission of the President, through the Secretary of the Treasury, or proceeding to any of said States, with the exceptions aforesaid, by land or water, together with the vessel or vehicle conveying the same, or conveying persons to or from said States, with said exceptions, will be forfeited to the United States; and that from and after fifteen days from the issuing of this proclamation, all ships and vessels belonging in whole or in part to any citizen or inhabitant of any of said States, with said exceptions, found at sea, or in any port of the United States, will be forfeited to the United States; and I hereby enjoin upon all district attorneys, marshals, and officers of the revenue and of the military and naval forces of the United States, to be vigilant in the execution of said act, and in the enforcement of the penalties and forfeitures imposed or declared by it; leaving any party who may think himself aggrieved thereby to his application to the Secretary of the Treasury for the remission of any penalty or forfeiture, which the said Secretary is authorized by law to grant if, in his judgment, the special circumstances of any case shall require such remission.

Proclamation of 1st January, 1863, commonly called the Emancipation Proclamation:

Whereas, on the twenty-second day of September, in the year of our Lord one thousand eight hundred and sixty-two, a proclamation was issued by the President of the United States, containing, among other things, the following, to wit:

"That on the first day of January, in the year of our Lord one thousand eight hundred and sixty-three, all persons held as slaves within any State or designated part of a State, the people whereof shall then be in rebellion against the United States, shall be then thenceforth and forever free, and the executive government of the United States, including the military and naval authority thereof, will recognize and maintain the freedom of such persons, and will do no act or acts to repress such persons or any of them in any effort they may make for their actual freedom. That the

Executive will, on the first day of January aforesaid, by proclamation, designate the States and parts of States, if any, in which the people therein respectively shall then be in rebellion against the United States, and the fact that any State or the people thereof shall on that day be in good faith represented in the Congress of the United States by members chosen thereto at elections wherein a majority of the qualified voters of such State shall have participated, shall, in the absence of strong countervailing testimony, be deemed conclusive evidence that such State and the people thereof are not then in rebellion against the United States."

Now, therefore, I, Abraham Lincoln, President of the United States, by virtue of the power in me vested as Commander-in-Chief of the army and navy of the United States, in time of actual armed rebellion against the authority and government of the United States, and as a fit and necessary war measure for suppressing said rebellion, do, on this first day of January, in the year of our Lord one thousand eight hundred and sixty-three, and in accordance with my purpose so to do publicly proclaimed for the full period of one hundred days from the day of the first above-mentioned order, designate as the States and parts of States wherein the people thereof respectively are this day in rebellion against the United States the following, to wit:

Arkansas.
Texas.
Louisiana — except the parishes of St. Bernard, Placquemines, Jefferson, St. John, St. Charles, St. James, Ascension, Assumption, Terre Bonne, Lafourche, St. Mary, St. Martin, and Orleans, including the city of New Orleans.
Mississippi.
Alabama.
Florida.
Georgia.
South Carolina.

North Carolina, and
Virginia—except the forty-eight counties designated as West Virginia, and also the counties of Berkley, Accomac, Northampton, Elizabeth City, York, Princess Ann, and Norfolk, including the cities of Norfolk and Portsmouth, and which excepted parts are, for the present, left precisely as if this proclamation were not issued.

And, by virtue of the power and for the purpose aforesaid, I do order and declare that all persons held as slaves within said designated States and parts of States are and henceforward shall be free; and that the executive government of the United States, including the military and naval authorities thereof, will recognize and maintain the freedom of said persons.

And I hereby enjoin upon the people so declared to be free to abstain from all violence unless in necessary self-defense, and I recommend to them that in all cases, when allowed, they labor faithfully for reasonable wages.

And I further declare and make known that such persons, of suitable condition, will be received into the armed service of the United States, to garrison forts, positions, stations, and other places, and to man vessels of all sorts in said service.

And, upon this, sincerely believed to be an act of justice, warranted by the Constitution, upon military necessity, I invoke the considerate judgment of mankind and the gracious favor of Almighty God.

Punishment of Treason, Confiscation, and Amnesty Act.

THE PRESIDENT'S "SIXTY DAYS' NOTICE."

In pursuance of the sixth section of the act of Congress, entitled "An act to suppress insurrection and to punish treason and rebellion, to seize and confiscate the property of rebels, and for other purposes," approved July 17, 1862, and which act and the joint resolution explanatory thereof are herewith published; I, Abraham Lincoln, President of the United States, do hereby proclaim to and warn all persons within the contemplation of said sixth section to cease participating in, aiding, countenancing, or abetting the existing rebellion, or any rebellion against the Government of the United States, and to return to their proper allegiance to the United States, on pain of the forfeitures and seizures as within and by said sixth section provided.

PROCLAMATION.

I, Abraham Lincoln, President of the United States of America, and Commander-in-Chief of the army and navy thereof, do hereby proclaim and declare that hereafter, as heretofore, the war will be prosecuted for the object of practically restoring the constitutional relation between the United States and the people thereof, in which States that relation is, or may be, suspended or disturbed; that it is my purpose upon the next meeting of Congress, to again recommend the adoption of a practical measure tendering pecuniary aid to the free acceptance or rejection of all the Slave States so called, the people whereof may not then be in rebellion against the United States, and which States may then have voluntarily adopted or thereafter may voluntarily adopt the immediate or gradual abolishment of slavery within their respective limits; and that the effort to colonize persons of African descent, with their consent, upon this continent or elsewhere, with the previously obtained consent of the governments existing there, will be continued; that on the first day of January, in the year of our Lord one thousand eight hundred and sixty-three, all persons held as slaves within any State, or any designated part of a State, the people whereof shall then be in rebellion against the United States, shall be thenceforward and forever free, and the Executive Government of the United States, including the military and naval authority thereof, will recognize and maintain the freedom of such persons, and will do no act or acts to repress such persons, or any of them, in any efforts they may make for their actual freedom; that the Executive will, on the first day of January aforesaid, by proclamation, designate the States and parts of States, if any, in which the people thereof respectively shall then be in rebellion against the United States, and the fact that any State, or the people thereof, shall on that day be in good faith represented in the Congress of the United States by members chosen thereto at elections wherein a majority of the qualified voters of such State shall have participated, shall, in the absence of strong countervailing testimony, be deemed conclusive evidence that such State and the people thereof are not then in rebellion against the United States.

That attention is hereby called to an act of Congress, entitled "An act to make an additional article of war, approved March 13, 1862, and which act is in the words and figures following:

Be it enacted by the Senate and House of Representatives of the United States of America in Congress assembled: That hereafter the following shall be promulgated as an additional article of war, for the government of the army of the United States, and shall be obeyed and observed as such:

Article. All officers or persons in the military or naval service of the United States are prohibited from employing any of the forces under their respective commands for the purpose of returning fugitives from service or labor, who may have escaped from any persons to whom such labor is claimed to be due, and any officer who shall be found guilty by a court-martial of violating this article, shall be dismissed from the service.

SEC. 2. *And be it further enacted,* That this act shall take effect from and after its passage.

Also, to the ninth and tenth sections of an act entitled "An act to suppress insurrection, to punish treason and rebellion, to seize and confiscate the property of rebels, and for other purposes," approved July 17, 1862, and which sections are in the words and figures following:

SEC. 9. *And be it further enacted,* That all slaves of persons who shall hereafter be engaged in rebellion against the Government of the United States, or who shall in any way give aid or comfort thereto, escaping from such persons and taking refuge within the lines of the army; and all slaves captured from such persons or deserted by them, and coming under the control of the Government of the United States; and all slaves of such persons found on (or being within) any place occupied by rebel forces and afterward occupied by the forces of the United States, shall be deemed captives of war, and shall be forever free of their servitude, and not again held as slaves.

SEC. 10. *And be it further enacted,* That no slave escaping into any State, Territory, or the District of Columbia, from any of the States, shall be delivered up, or in any way impeded or hindered of his liberty, except for crime or some offense against the laws, unless the person claiming said fugitive shall first make oath that the person to whom the labor or service of such fugitive is alleged to be due, is his lawful owner, and has not been in arms against the United States in the present rebellion, nor in any way given aid and comfort thereto; and no person engaged in the military or naval service of the United States shall, under any pretense whatever, assume to decide on the validity of the claim of any person to the service or labor of any other person, or render up any such person to the claimant, on pain of being dismissed from the service.

And I do hereby enjoin upon and order all persons engaged in the military and naval service of the United States to observe, obey, and enforce, within their respective spheres of service, the act and sections above recited.

And the Executive will in due time recommend that all citizens of the United States who shall have remained loyal thereto throughout the rebellion, shall (upon the restoration of the constitutional relation between the United States and their respective States and people, if the relation shall have been suspended or disturbed) be compensated for all losses by acts of the United States, including the loss of slaves.

STATISTICAL TABLES BEARING ON THE CIVIL WAR.

REAL ESTATE AND PERSONAL PROPERTY, 1850 AND 1860.

States and Territories.	Real Estate and Personal Property. 1850.	1860.	Increase.	Increase per cent.
California	$22,161,872	$207,874,618	$185,712,741	837.98
Connecticut	155,707,980	444,274,114	288,566,134	185.32
Delaware	21,062,556	46,242,181	25,179,625	119.54
Illinois	156,265,006	871,860.282	715.595,276	457.93
Indiana	202,650,264	528,835,371	326,185.107	160.95
Iowa	23,714,638	247,338,265	223,623,627	942.97
Kansas	—	31,327,895	—	—
Kentucky	301,628,456	666,043,112	364,414,656	120.81
Maine	122,777,571	190,211,600	67,434,029	54.92
Maryland	219,217,364	376,919,944	157,702,580	71.93
Massachusetts	573,342,286	815,237,433	241,895,147	42.19
Michigan	59,787,255	257,163,983	197,376,728	330.13
Minnesota	Not returned.	52,294,413	—	—
Missouri	137,247,707	501,214,898	363,966,691	265.18
New Hampshire	103,652,835	156,310,860	52,658,025	50.80
New Jersey*	200,000,000	467,918,324	267,918,324	133.95
New York	1,080,309,216	1,843,358,517	763,029,301	70.63
Ohio	504,726,120	1,193,898,422	689,172,302	136.54
Oregon	5,063,474	28,930,637	23,867,163	471.35
Pennsylvania	722,486,120	1,416,501,818	694,015,698	96.05
Rhode Island	80,508,794	135,337,588	54,828,794	68.10
Vermont	92,205.049	122,477,170	30,272,121	32.83
Wisconsin	42,056,595	273,671,668	231,615,073	550.72
Loyal States	4,826,571,158	10,875,222,608	6,048,651,450	125.32
Alabama	228,204.332	495,237,078	267,032,746	117.01
Arkansas	89,841,025	219,256,473	179,415,448	450.32
Florida	22,862,270	73,101,500	50,239,230	219.74
Georgia	335,425,714	645,895,237	310,469,523	92.56
Louisiana	233,998,764	602,118,568	368,119,804	157.31
Mississippi	228,951.130	607,324,911	378,373,781	165.26
North Carolina	226,800,472	358,739,399	131,938,927	58.17
South Carolina	288,257,694	548,138,754	259,881,060	90.15
Tennessee	201,246,686	493,903,892	292,657,206	145.42
Texas	52,740,473	365,200,614	312,460,141	592.44
Virginia	430,701,082	793,249,681	362,548,599	84.17
Seceded States	2,289,029,650	5,202,166,107	2,913,136,457	127.26
District of Columbia	14,018.874	41,084,945	27,066,071	193.06
Nebraska Territory	—	9,131,056	—	—
New Mexico Territory	5,174,471	20,813,768	15,639,298	302.24
Utah Territory	986.083	5,596,118	4,610,035	467.50
Washington Territory	—	5,601,466	—	—
Aggregate U. S.	7,135,780,228	16,159,616,068	8,925,481,011	126.45

* Partly estimated.

POPULATION AND REPRESENTATION.

States and Territories.	Area sq. m.	Population 1860. White.	Free Colored.	Slave.	Total.	Representative Population.	39th Congress.
California	188,982	375,908	4,086	—	379,994	379,994	3
Connecticut	4,674	451,520	8,627	—	460,147	460,147	4
Delaware	2,120	90,589	19,829	1,798	112,216	111,496	1
Illinois	55,405	1,704,323	7,628	—	1,711,951	1,711,951	*14
Indiana	33,809	1,339,000	11,428	—	1,350,428	1,350,428	*11
Iowa	55,044	673,844	1,069	—	674,913	674,913	*6
Kansas	78,418	106,579	625	2	107,206	107,206	1
Kentucky	37,680	919,517	10,684	225,483	1,155,684	1,065,490	*9
Maine	31,766	626,952	1,327	—	628,279	628,279	5
Maryland	11,124	515,918	83,942	87,189	687,049	652,173	5
Massachusetts	7,800	1,221,464	9,602	—	1,231,066	1,231,066	10
Michigan	56,243	742,314	6,799	—	749,113	749,113	6
Minnesota	83,531	171,864	259	—	172,123	172,123	*2
Missouri	67,380	1,063,509	3,572	114,931	1,182,012	1,136,039	9
New Hampshire	9,280	325,579	494	—	326,073	326,073	3
New Jersey	8,320	646,699	25,318	18	672,035	672,027	5
New York	47,000	3,831,730	49,005	—	3,880,735	3,880,735	31
Ohio	39,964	2,302,838	36,673	—	2,339,511	2,339,511	*19
Oregon	95,274	52,337	128	—	52,465	52,465	1
Pennsylvania	46,000	2,849,266	56,849	—	2,906,115	2,906,115	*24
Rhode Island	1,306	170,668	3,952	—	174,620	174,620	*2
Vermont	10,212	314,389	709	—	315,098	315,098	*3
Wisconsin	53,924	774,710	1,171	—	775,881	775,881	6
Loyal States	1,025,257	21,271,517	343,776	429,421	22,044,714	21,862,946	180

Alabama	50,722	526,431	2,690	435,080	964,201	790,169	6
Arkansas	52,198	324,191	144	111,115	435,450	391,004	3
Florida	59,268	77,748	952	61,745	140,425	115,727	1
Georgia	52,009	591,588	3,500	462,198	1,057,286	872 406	7
Louisiana	46,431	357,629	18,647	331,726	708,002	575,311	5
Mississippi	47,156	353,901	773	436,631	791,305	616,652	5
North Carolina	50,704	631,100	30,463	331,059	992,622	860,198	7
South Carolina	29,385	291,388	9,914	402,406	703,708	542,745	4
Tennessee	45,600	826,782	7,300	275,719	1,109,801	999,513	8
Texas	237,504	421,294	355	182,566	604,215	531,188	4
Virginia†	61,352	1,047,411	58,042	490,865	1,596,318	1,399,972	11
Seceded States	732,329	5,449,463	132,760	3,521,110	9,103,338	7,694,889	61
TOTAL STATES	1,757,586	26,720,980	476,536	3,950,531	31,148,047	29,557,835	241
Colorado	105,818	34,231	46	—	34,277		
Dakota	318,128	4,837	—	—	4,837		
Nebraska	122,007	28,759	67	15	28,841		
Nevada	73,473	6,812	45	—	6,857		
New Mexico	243,063	93,431	85	—	93,516		
Utah	128,835	40,214	30	29	40,273		
Washington	175,141	11,564	30	—	11,594		
TOTAL TERRITORIES	1,166,465	219,848	303	44	220,195		
DISTRICT OF COLUMBIA	60	60,764	11,131	3,185	75,080		
TOTAL ORGANIZED	2,924,111	27,001,592	487,970	3,953,760	31,443,322		
Indian Territory	76,891	1,988	404	7,369	9,761		
Tribal Indians	—	—	—	—	294,431		
GRAND TOTAL	3,001,002	27,003,580	488,374	3,961,129	31,747,514		

[The apportionment under the census of 1860 gave each of the States marked thus (*) one member less than set down in the table. The supplemental member was added by a special act of Congress, passed 4th March, 1862.]

☞ Chinese, half-breeds, and civil Indians are reckoned as white persons.

☞ The representative number was 126,856.

† See West Virginia, p. 160; deduct population from Seceded States, and add to Loyal States.

POPULAR VOTE FOR PRESIDENT, 1860.

States.	Lincoln (Republican).	Douglas (Democrat).	Breckinridge (Democrat).	Bell (Union).
California	39,173	38,516	34,334	6,817
Connecticut	43,792	15,522	14,641	*3,291
Delaware	3,815	1,023	7,337	3,864
Illinois	172,161	160,215	2,404	4,913
Indiana	139,033	115,509	12,295	5,306
Iowa	70,409	55,111	1,048	1,763
Kentucky	1,364	25,651	53,143	66,058
Maine	62,811	26,693	6,368	2,046
Maryland	2,294	5,966	42,482	41,760
Massachusetts	106,533	34,372	5,939	22,331
Michigan	88,480	65,057	805	405
Minnesota	22,069	11,920	748	62
Missouri	17,028	58,801	31,317	58,372
New Hampshire	37,519	25,881	2,112	441
New Jersey	58,324	*62,801	—	—
New York	353,804	*303,329	—	—
Ohio	231,610	187,232	11,405	12,194
Oregon	5,270	3,951	5,006	183
Pennsylvania	268,030	16,765	*178,871	12,776
Rhode Island	12,244	*7,707	—	—
Vermont	33,808	6,849	218	1,969
Wisconsin	86,110	65,021	888	161
Loyal States	1,855,681	1,293,892	411,361	244,712
Alabama	—	13,651	48,831	27,875
Arkansas	—	5,227	28,732	20,094
Florida	—	367	8,543	5,437
Georgia	—	11,590	51,889	42,886
Louisiana	—	7,625	22,681	20,204
Mississippi	—	3,283	40,797	25,040
North Carolina	—	2,701	48,539	44,990
South Carolina	(*Electors chosen by Legislature.*)			
Tennessee	—	11,350	64,709	69,274
Texas	—	—	47,548	*15,438
Virginia	1,929	16,290	74,323	74,681
Seceded States	1,929	72,084	436,592	345,919
Grand Total	1,857,610	1,365,976	847,953	590,631

* Fusion.

COST OF THE WAR.

ACTUAL COST FOR 1861 AND 1862, AND ESTIMATED FOR 1863 AND 1864.

(Compiled from the Reports of the Treasury Department.)

	1861.	1862.	1863.	1864.
EXPENDITURES.				
War Department	$22,981,150 44	$394,368,407 36	$747,359,828 98	$738,829,146 80
Navy Department	12,428,577 09	42,674,569 61	82,177,510 77	68,257,255 01
Civil List	23,187,203 19	21,408,491 16	32,811.543 23	25,081,510 08
Pensions and Indians	3,760,022 72	3,102,985 50	5,982,906 43	10,346,577 01
Interest on debt	4,000,173 76	13,190,324 45	25,014,532 07	33,513,890 50
Loans and debt redeemed	18,221,707 27	96,096,922 09	95,212,456 14	19,384,804 16
Balance undrawn	2,257,065 80	13,043,546 81	—	200,000,000 00
Total expenditures	$86,835,900 27	$583,885,247 06	$788,558,777 62	$1,095,413,183 56
RECEIPTS.				
Customs	39,582,125 64	49,056,397 62	68,041,736 59	70,000,000 00
Public lands	870,658 54	152,203 77	88,724 06	25,000 00
Direct tax	—	1,795,331 73	11,620,717 99	—
Internal revenue	—	—	85,456,303 73	150,000,000 00
Miscellaneous	892,199 64	931,787 64	2,244,316 32	3,000,000 00
From loans	41,861,709 74	529,692,460 50	608,063,432 02	622,388,183 56
Balances on hand	3,629,206 71	2,257,065 80	13,043,546 81	250,000,000 00
Total receipts	$86,835,900 27	$583,885,247 06	$788,558,777 62	$1,095,413,183 56

THE PUBLIC DEBT OF THE UNITED STATES:

On the 1st day of July, 1861, was	$90,867,828	On the 1st day of July, 1863, will be	$1,024,497,725
On the 1st day of July, 1862, was	511,646,274	On the 1st day of July, 1864, will be	1,627,501,105

STATE OF WEST VIRGINIA.

ADMITTED INTO THE UNION 31ST DECEMBER, 1862.

Counties.	Whites.	Free Col.	Slaves.	Total.	County Seats.
Barbour	8,728	135	95	8,958	Philippi.
Boone	4,681	1	158	4,840	Ballardsville.
Braxton	4,885	3	104	4,992	Sutton.
Brooke	5,425	51	18	5,494	Wellsburg.
Cabell	7,691	24	305	8,020	Barboursville.
Calhoun	2,492	1	9	2,502	Arnoldsburg.
Clay	1,761	5	21	1,787	Clay C. H.
Doddridge	5,168	1	34	5,203	West Union.
Fayette	5,716	10	271	5,997	Fayetteville.
Gilmer	3,685	22	52	3,759	Glenville.
Greenbrier	10,500	186	1,525	12,211	Lewisburg.
Hampshire	12,478	222	1,213	13,913	Romney.
Hancock	4,442	1	2	4,445	Hancock.
Hardy	8,521	270	1,073	9,864	Moorefield.
Harrison	13,176	32	582	13,790	Clarksburg.
Jackson	8,240	11	55	8,306	Ripley.
Kanawha	13,785	181	2,184	16,150	Charleston.
Lewis	7,736	33	230	7,999	Weston.
Logan	4,789	1	148	4,938	Arracoma.
McDowell	1,535	—	—	1,535	Gilead Spring.
Marion	12,656	3	63	12,722	Fairmount.
Marshall	12,911	57	29	12,997	Moundsville.
Mason	8,750	47	376	9,173	Point Pleasan
Mercer	6,428	29	362	6,819	Princeton.
Monongalia	12,901	46	101	13,048	Morgantown.
Monroe	9,536	107	1,114	10,757	Union.
Morgan	3,614	24	94	3,732	Bath.
Nicholas	4,471	2	154	4,627	Summersville.
Ohio	22,196	126	100	22,422	Wheeling.
Pendleton	5,870	50	244	6,164	Franklin.
Pleasants	2,925	5	15	2,945	St. Mary's.
Pocahontas	3,686	20	252	3,958	Huntersville.
Preston	13,200	45	67	13,312	Kingwood.
Putnam	5,708	13	580	6,301	Putnam.
Raleigh	3,291	19	57	3,367	Beckley.
Randolph	4,793	14	183	4,990	Beverly.
Ritchie	6,809	—	38	6,847	Harrisville.
Roane	5,307	2	72	5,381	Roane C. H.
Taylor	7,300	51	112	7,463	Pruntytown.
Tucker	1,392	16	20	1,428	St. George.
Tyler	6,488	11	18	6,517	Middlebourne.
Upshur	7,064	16	212	7.292	Buckhannon.
Wayne	6,604	—	143	6,747	Trout's Hill.
Webster	1,552	—	3	1,555	Webster C. H
Wetzel	6,691	2	10	6,703	New Martinsville.
Wirt	3,728	—	23	3,751	Elizabeth.
Wood	10,791	79	176	11,046	Parkersburg.
Wyoming	2,795	2	64	2,861	Oceana.
Total State	334,891	2,246	12,761	349,698	WHEELING.

www.ingramcontent.com/pod-product-compliance
Lightning Source LLC
LaVergne TN
LVHW021405110826
845150LV00007B/1789

* 9 7 8 1 4 2 5 5 1 2 8 8 0 *